Careers in Focus

Food

Ferguson Publishing Company
Chicago, Illinois

Editorial Staff

Andrew Morkes, *Managing Editor-Career Publications*
Carol Yehling, *Senior Editor*
Anne Paterson, *Editor*
Nora Walsh, *Editor*

Library of Congress Cataloging-in-Publication Data

Careers in focus : Food.-- 2nd ed.
     p. cm.
Includes index.
 ISBN 0-89434-441-2
 1. Food service--Vocational guidance. 2. Food industry and trade--Vocational guidance.
I. Title: Food. II. Ferguson Publishing Company.
TX911.3.V62 C38 2003
647.95'023--dc21

                              2002009200

Printed in the United States of America

Cover photo courtesy Ken Hammond, U.S. Department of Agriculture

Published and distributed by
Ferguson Publishing Company
200 West Jackson Boulevard, 7th Floor
Chicago, Illinois 60606
800-306-9941
www.fergpubco.com

Z-8

JUN _ - 2005

Table of Contents

Introduction

The food industry is the largest single industry in the United States and throughout the world. It begins with the farmers who cultivate the land, raise livestock, and grow plants. Although wheat and corn are the primary crops in this country, farmers grow nearly every kind of grain, fruit, vegetable, seed, and plant we eat. Livestock production centers primarily on cattle, poultry, and pigs, but American farmers also raise sheep, goats, turkeys, and fish. After crops are harvested or livestock is bred, a number of industries store, ship, process, and package the farmer's yield.

Food processors or manufacturers stand in the middle of the food industry production line. They work with farmers, research laboratories, wholesalers and retailers who distribute their finished products, and consumers who buy them. There is an enormous variety of methods for preparing food. Some foods may require only one preparation method; others may require several. Lettuce usually just needs to be harvested and washed, but some companies now offer packaged lettuce, often with bits of carrots and red cabbage, as ready-to-eat salad. Cows and other animals are slaughtered, cleaned, and cut up for consumption. Foods for frozen dinners require a great deal of preparation. They need to be harvested, cleaned, combined, and cooked according to a recipe, portioned out, and then frozen in special packaging.

Food processing prevents food from spoiling as quickly as it would otherwise. It also provides greater convenience, variety, color, taste, and, in many cases, monetary savings. Food is processed and preserved by cold storage, canning, freezing, drying, freeze-drying, curing, and, most recently, by the use of antibiotics and a process called irradiation, which uses microwave and ultraviolet rays.

After food is cleaned, processed, and packaged, it goes to various markets, such as grocery stores and restaurants and other food service outlets. According to the Food Marketing Institute, 3.5 million people work in the grocery industry. Some of those workers are at the corporate level, while others work in the 127,000 stores. Consumers make an average of 2.3 trips to the grocery each week, spending about 7.1 percent of their weekly income on food. With more than 49,000 items to choose from in a typical supermarket, American consumers are accustomed to the variety and convenience of grocery stores.

The food service industry is strong and rapidly growing. Restaurants, coffee shops, fast food chains, food outlets in catering firms, hotels, hospitals, and other institutions are all part of this segment of the food industry. Employees working in the front of the restaurant include wait staff, host staff, maitre d's, and bartenders. They have the important responsibility of presenting prepared meals directly to their customers. Those in the back of the house include salad and sandwich makers, cooks, and chefs at different levels and with different specialties.

More than 25 percent of all people working in the United States are employed in some part of the food industry, making it one of the country's largest areas of employment. The food industry grew from $46 billion a year in 1950 to about $280 billion in the early 1980s. By 1999, that figure reached $486 billion.

Careers in farming are expected to grow more slowly than the average. Farmers and other workers in agriculture are increasingly using high-tech methods of conservation, planting, tilling, and treating crops, as well as developing ways to breed and raise livestock.

The food processing industry faces challenges in several areas, especially food product labeling, food packaging, and increasing the nutritional value in processed foods. Many production jobs are slowly being phased out as automation has made the processing of many types of food both more efficient and more cost-effective. Jobs that do not require special skills are expected to decline over the next decade as more and more companies introduce computerized machinery.

The outlook for employment in the grocery industry is slower than the average, according to the U.S. Department of Labor. The number of grocery stores has decreased by 19.2 percent in the past 10 years, but sales have continued to increase. Approximately 2.9 million people worked in the grocery industry in 1986; the industry provided 3.1 million wage and salary jobs in 2000. While technological advances have decreased employment in other industries, the technological improvements in the grocery industry still require real people to be present. Online grocery stores are new, and at present, account for only a small percentage of sales in the grocery industry. However, sales are expected to continue to grow, which could create a need for more delivery and technical personnel in those companies.

Slightly better-than-average job growth is expected for restaurant and food service managers; chefs, cooks, and other kitchen workers; and food and beverage service workers. The number of food service managers is expected to grow 24.7 percent through 2010. The number of back-of-the-house employees is anticipated to increase, with the exception of fast-food and short-order cooks. And front-of-the-house workers also will enjoy faster than average job growth.

Each article in this book discusses a particular food industry occupation in detail. The information comes from Ferguson's *Encyclopedia of Careers and Vocational Guidance*. The **Overview** section is a brief introductory description of the duties and responsibilities of a person in the career. Oftentimes, a career may have a variety of job titles. When this is the case, alternative career titles are presented in this section. The **History** section describes the history of the particular job as it relates to the overall development of its industry or field. The **Job** describes the primary and secondary duties of the job. **Requirements** discusses high school and post-secondary education and training requirements, any certification or licensing necessary, and any other personal requirements for success in the job. **Exploring** offers suggestions on how to gain some experience in or knowledge of the particular job before making a firm educational and financial commitment. The focus is on what can be done while still in high school (or in the early years of college) to gain a better understanding of the job. The **Employers** section gives an overview of typical places of employment for the job. **Starting Out** discusses the best ways to land that first job, be it through the college placement office, newspaper ads, or personal contact. The **Advancement** section describes what kind of career path to expect from the job and how to get there. **Earnings** lists salary ranges and describes the typical fringe benefits. The **Work Environment** section describes the typical surroundings and conditions of employment—whether indoors or outdoors, noisy or quiet, social or independent, and so on. Also discussed are typical hours worked, any seasonal fluctuations, and the stresses and strains of the job. The **Outlook** section summarizes the job in terms of the general economy and industry projections. For the most part, Outlook information is obtained from the Bureau of Labor Statistics and is supplemented by information taken from professional associations. Job growth terms follow those used in the *Occupational Outlook Handbook.* Growth described as "much faster than the average" means an increase of 36 percent or more. Growth described as "faster than the average" means an increase of 21 to 35 percent. Growth described as "about as fast as the average" means an increase of 10 to 20 percent. Growth described as "little change or more slowly than the average" means an increase of 0 to 9 percent. "Decline" means a decrease of 1 percent or more.

Each article ends with **For More Information,** which lists organizations that can provide career information on training, education, internships, scholarships, and job placement.

Bakery Workers

Overview

Bakery workers are the many different professionals who work to produce bread, cakes, biscuits, pies, pastries, crackers, and other baked goods in commercial, institutional, and industrial bakeries. Approximately 66,000 food batchmakers are employed in manufacturing settings to tend equipment that mixes, blends, and cooks, and approximately 160,000 bakers are employed in such places as grocery stores, specialty shops, and manufacturing.

History

Baking, the process of cooking food using dry heat, is perhaps the oldest method of cooking. The ancient Egyptians are credited with building the first known ovens, which were shaped like beehives and made of clay from the banks of the Nile River. Later cultures introduced various technological improvements, including the Roman cylindrical oven. By the middle of the second century BC, there were professional bakers in Rome, and ordinary people could buy bread instead of having to make it themselves. The first mechanical dough mixer, powered by a horse or donkey walking in circles, was built by the Romans. In European cities during the Middle Ages, bakers formed associations called guilds, which carefully regulated how bread was made and how bakers were trained. Outside of cities, however, most baking was done at home or in a single village oven.

Professional bakers were common in colonial America, but most settlers in small communities baked bread at home. The beginnings of an industrial society changed the American idea of self-sufficiency. Urban workers and apartment dwellers did not always have the time or facilities to make their own baked goods. Technology made possible huge ovens, mixers, and ways of controlling heat and measurements that enabled manufacturers to make mass quantities of good baked food at reasonable prices.

In recent years, the popularity of bread machines has led more and more people to bake their own bread. Most Americans, however, still buy bread and other baked goods at the grocery store or from retail bakeries. Manufactured cookies and crackers are found on the shelves of nearly every American kitchen. The freshness, taste, and consistency of these products are the responsibility of bakery workers.

The Job

Most bakery workers working for manufacturers (for example, a large company that produces hamburger buns or coffee cakes, which are eventually sold in the neighborhood grocery store) participate in only some of the stages involved in creating a baked item. These workers, or food batchmakers, are usually designated by the type of machine they operate or the stage of baking with which they are involved.

In preparing the dough or batter for goods baked in an industrial bakery, different workers make the different components. *Blenders* tend machines that blend flour. Skilled technicians known as *broth mixers* control flour sifters and various vats to measure and mix liquid solutions for fermenting, oxidizing, and shortening. These solutions consist of such ingredients as yeast, sugar, shortening, and enriching ingredients mixed with water or milk. The broth mixer must carefully control the temperature of the broth; if it is just a few degrees too hot or too cool, the dough or batter will not rise properly. The broth mixer runs these solutions through a heat regulator and into dough-mixing machines.

Batter mixers tend machines that mix ingredients for batters for cakes and other products. These workers must select and install mixing utensils in huge mixers, depending on the kind of batter to be mixed. They regulate the speed and time of mixing and check the consistency of the batter.

Other kinds of mixers and shapers include *unleavened-dough mixers*, who use a five-position mixer to make matzo; *sweet-goods-machine operators*, who roll and cut sweet dough to make rolls and other sweet products; and *pretzel twisters*, who form pretzel shapes out of dough by hand or machine. *Cracker-and-cookie-machine operators* roll dough into sheets and form crackers or cookies before baking. They check the machine's work and remove any malformed items before baking. *Wafer-machine operators* perform similar tasks with wafer batter. *Batter scalers* operate machines that deposit measured amounts of batter on conveyors. *Doughnut makers* and *doughnut-machine operators* mix batter, shape, and fry doughnuts. Some workers operate machines that grease baking pans or that place pie-crusts and fillings into pie plates for baking.

Bakery helpers have general duties such as greasing pans, moving supplies, measuring dump materials, and cleaning equipment. Bakery helpers sit at benches or conveyor belts, where they may fill, enrobe, slice, package, seal, stack, or count baked goods.

When baked goods are ready for delivery and sale, *bakery checkers* prorate and distribute baked goods to *route-sales drivers*, who deliver products to customers and try to drum up new business or increase business along their routes. Bakeries also employ *bakery-maintenance engineers*, also called *bakery-machine mechanics* or *plant mechanics*, to keep the many mixers, ovens, and other machines in good order.

Bakery supervisors, who work in industrial bakeries, are sometimes assisted by *bakers* or *all-around bakers* in overseeing production. Bakers and all-around bakers, however, most frequently work in small businesses, hotels, or restaurants where they develop recipes and mix, shape, bake, and finish baked goods.

Bread and pastry bakers, also known as *pastry chefs*, also work in restaurants, small businesses, such as the neighborhood bakery shop, and institutions, such as schools. Unlike bakery workers employed in industrial settings, these bakers and chefs often do much of their work by hand. They may have a fair amount of independence in deciding what items and how much of them to produce. Creativity is needed, especially when decorating an item made for a special occasion, such as a birthday cake for Billy or a wedding cake for John and Jane.

Requirements

HIGH SCHOOL

Many bakers begin as bakery helpers. Most employers prefer to hire high school graduates. Classes that will help you in this field include family and consumer science, which should teach you about food preparation, health, to learn about nutrition, and math, such as algebra and geometry, so that you are comfortable using numbers and making calculations. You may also want to take science courses such as biology and chemistry to get an understanding of substances' properties and reactions. If you are interested in working as a bakery-maintenance engineer, take shop classes that will teach you to work with electricity and machinery.

POSTSECONDARY TRAINING

Some bakery workers acquire useful skills through education in technical schools or in the U.S. Armed Forces. However, they usually complete their education on the job.

The skills that bakery helpers need to become bakers in wholesale baking plants can be learned in several ways. In some companies, bakery helpers learn through formal apprenticeships. Apprenticeships consist of a blend of classroom and on-the-job instruction and take several years to complete.

After they have some experience, bakery workers who have proved they are good employees but want to upgrade their skills may attend training courses offered by the American Institute of Baking. Others take correspondence courses and seminars offered by the American Institute of Baking at various locations. Bakers who successfully complete this training receive specialty certification in bread, cake, or cracker production.

Some chef training schools have bakery programs for students interested in learning diverse baking skills, from basic bread to gourmet pastries.

Some companies provide apprenticeships for employees who are training to be bakery-maintenance engineers. Another option is to take classes, correspondence courses, and seminars offered by the American Institute of Baking.

Bakery workers may belong to the Bakery, Confectionery, and Tobacco Workers International Union. Route drivers may belong to the International Brotherhood of Teamsters, Chauffeurs, Warehousemen, and Helpers of America.

CERTIFICATION OR LICENSING

As mentioned in the previous section, the American Institute of Baking offers courses leading to certification in a number of areas. Designations that bakery workers can earn include Certified Baker—Bread and Rolls, Certified Baker—Cookies and Crackers, and Certified Maintenance Technician. Some employers may require certification; in other cases, certification is recommended for those wanting to advance their careers. In addition, most states require bakery workers to pass a physical exam and have a health certificate stating that they are free from contagious diseases.

OTHER REQUIREMENTS

Manual dexterity is important in many bakery jobs. Artistic ability is useful for those who enjoy decorating cakes, cookies, dough-nuts, and other baked goods. Bakery workers must also be able to work well as part of a team, since they are all contributing some-thing to create the finished products. Additionally, as with any professional working with food, they should have keen senses of smell and taste.

Exploring

While in high school, you may be able to get a part-time or summer job at a neighborhood bakery. Although you may only be responsible for taking customers' orders and ringing up sales, you will be able to experience working in this environment. In addition to school courses, take baking or cooking classes that are offered locally by community centers, grocery stores, or tech schools. Ask your guidance counselor to help you arrange for a tour of a local bakery and talk to workers about their jobs. If there is a cooking school in your area, visit it and meet with the teachers to discuss this line of work.

Employers

Bakery workers can find jobs in a wide variety of settings, from small retail bakeries and bakery departments in supermarkets to multinational companies with huge manufacturing plants. They also may work in wholesale bakeries or distribution centers as well as in restaurants and hotels.

Starting Out

Aspiring bakers can apply to bakeries for jobs as helpers or apprentices. Students can often find jobs or apprenticeships through placement offices at baking schools. State employment offices and newspapers may provide leads. Local unions also have information about job openings.

Advancement

Helpers who learn machine-operator skills may move into these positions, but usually only after years of experience. Because bakeries use many different kinds of machines and processes, versatile workers are the most likely to be promoted. Skilled machine operators can move into supervisory slots or become all-around bakers. These bakers may also move into work in hotels, restaurants, or retail bakeries. They may even open their own bakeries and bake their goods by hand.

Some experienced bakery workers can be promoted into management positions. The trend, however, is to fill management slots in bakeries with people who have college degrees in management or other business fields. Route-sales drivers may work into sales manager positions or become route supervisors.

Earnings

The salary range for bakers and food batchmakers is wide due to factors such as size and type of employer, the employee's experience, and job position. According to the U.S. Department of Labor, the median yearly earnings for all bakers were $19,710 in 2000. Median yearly earnings for bakers working in the bakery products industry, however, were $23,010; those in the grocery store industry, $19,220; and those in retail bakeries, $18,060. The highest paid 10 percent of all bakers, regardless of industry, made more than $31,720 in 2000, and the lowest paid 10 percent earned less than $13,170 annually. The U.S. Department of Labor also reports that food batchmakers had median annual earnings of $20,990 in 2000.

Bakery workers who are members of a union generally earn more and have better job security than those who are not. Most bakery workers are eligible for overtime pay and premium pay for weekend work. Route drivers often work on commission, receiving base pay plus a percentage of their sales. Workers in apprentice positions are normally paid less than the full wages of experienced employees. In addition to regular pay, employees often receive benefits such as paid vacations and holidays, health insurance, and pension plans.

Work Environment

Bakery workers usually work 40 hours a week, and some work night and evening shifts. Because baked goods can be frozen until they are needed, the number of plants operating around the clock is less than it used to be.

Some bakery plants are air-conditioned. All are clean, since bakeries must meet state and federal standards. Bakery employees wear uniforms and caps or hairnets for sanitary reasons. Machines can be noisy, and working near ovens can be hot. Some jobs are strenuous, requiring heavy lifting.

Those in a small bakery may find they must work early morning hours in order to have freshly baked goods ready for customers when the shop opens. They may spend much of their time on their feet and have a fair amount of interaction with the public.

Outlook

The U.S. Department of Labor predicts that increasingly automated equipment and processes will result in an employment outlook of little change for food batchmakers and bakers in manufacturing. However, there may be a slight increase in the need for bakers at retail locations because of the growing number of traditional bakeries and specialty shops, such as cookie, muffin, and bagel shops. Overall, the department predicts growth at a rate slower than the average through 2010 for all workers in this field. Many current positions will become available as workers retire or change jobs.

For More Information

This organization represents the baking industry before the U.S. Congress and government regulatory agencies. It has industry information, including a salary survey.
AMERICAN BAKERS ASSOCIATION
1350 Eye Street, NW, Suite 1290
Washington, DC 20005
Tel: 202-789-0300
Web: http://www.americanbakers.org

For information on scholarships, online courses, and employment opportunities, contact:
AMERICAN INSTITUTE OF BAKING
1213 Bakers Way
Manhattan, KS 66502
Tel: 785-537-4750, 800-633-5137
Web: http://www.aibonline.org

This organization has industry information for the public and career information available to members.
AMERICAN SOCIETY OF BAKERY ENGINEERS
1200 Central Avenue, Suite 360
Wilmette, IL 60091
Web: http://www.asbe.org

Beverage Industry Workers

Overview

Beverage industry workers are located throughout the United States, manufacturing and bottling (or otherwise packaging) soft drinks, including carbonated beverages, coffee, tea, juices, and more recently, mineral and spring waters, also called "designer waters."

In addition to major locations where manufacturing, research and development, and administrative work are performed, many companies have smaller sites for bottling and distribution. Thus there are a variety of sites for larger companies as well as small, local manufacturers.

History

According to the National Soft Drink Association in Washington, DC, the manufacturing of soft drinks in America began in the 1830s. However, the evolution of soft drinks took place over a much longer time period. The forerunners of soft drinks began more than 2,000 years ago when Hippocrates, the "Father of Medicine," first suspected that mineral waters could be beneficial to our well-being.

In America, the transition resulted from the discovery of the natural springs in New York. Scientists began studying the tiny bubbles fizzing from these waters—carbon dioxide. They perfected a way to produce artificially carbonated water in the laboratory.

By the 1830s, pharmacists began to add ingredients from plants in an effort to improve the curative properties of soft drinks. Ginger ale, root beer, sarsaparilla, lemon, and strawberry were popular early flavors.

For many years, soft drinks were mixed in local pharmacies, but demand grew for them to be consumed in the home. Methods of bottling carbonated drinks were developed and in 1892 the "crown cap" was invented. It revolutionized the soft drink industry by preventing the escape of carbon dioxide from bottled beverages. Retail outlets began carrying the bottled drinks and the invention of "Hom-Paks," the first six-pack carton, made it more convenient to carry products home.

The Job

The beverage industry provides jobs in many phases of manufacturing, from mixing syrups for soft drinks to working on assembly lines for bottling, sealing, shipping, distributing, and selling the products. Plant, distribution, and sales managers are a few of the administrative positions, while maintenance, shipping, and technical workers are employed by most companies. There are many small companies involved at the bottling and wholesale level, where workers process, sell, and distribute beverages.

Plants that process soft drinks require workers who control flows, pressures, temperatures, line speeds, carbonation, Brix (measurement of sugar solution), and in-line blending.

Workers may be employed in growing and harvesting beverage industry products, such as coffee, tea, citrus, and other fruits, as well as the processing, packaging, shipping, distribution, and sales of these products.

Since many teas and coffees are imported from other countries, there are positions involving importing, processing, packaging, shipping, and distributing these products as well as in sales. There also are jobs in plants that create the sweeteners, syrups, bottles, cans, labels, and other items that support the manufacturing and sale of beverages.

In all areas of the beverage industry, positions range from unskilled laborers to highly paid administrative and sales staff.

There also are many technical and scientific positions, where people work to create new types of beverages, new flavors, and new packaging as well as in quality control. In 2001 the Food and Drug Administration announced a final rule on juice processors' need to comply with HACCP (Hazardous and Critical Control Point) principles to ensure safe production of juices. The purpose of the HACCP system is to eliminate illness-causing microbes and other hazards in the manufacturing process. To comply with the regulation, the industry began adding additional staff who have appropriate education and training in these areas. Still another area of employment related to the beverage industry is the recycling of cans and bottles.

Requirements

HIGH SCHOOL
A high school degree is required for many positions in the beverage industry, but that is only the beginning of preparation for this work. Courses in cooking, chemistry, shop, mathematics, and business will help prepare students for both the job itself and further training that is required in this complex and multilayered field. Although there are almost always some positions available for unskilled laborers, it is unlikely that any advancement or job security can be obtained without at least a high school diploma. Much training is provided by beverage companies, but basic education is necessary to qualify for more sophisticated training programs.

POSTSECONDARY TRAINING
Training as a laboratory technician can be advantageous in obtaining work in the beverage industry. An associate's degree also is helpful, but more education is required for many positions.

If you want to work in a management, supervisory, or quality control position, you will need at the minimum a college degree. Typical majors for those working in these areas include the sciences (biology and chemistry), engineering, or business. In addition, you will need to gain the applied skills and knowledge needed to manage a high-volume plant from in-house training, experience, and organizations, such as the International Society of Beverage Technologists (ISBT). ISBT, in conjunction with Florida

International University, offers training workshops and seminars covering technical subjects related to the beverage industry. In addition, ISBT technical committees present papers or seminars on topics such as sanitation, packaging, and health and safety at the organization's annual meetings.

OTHER REQUIREMENTS

More scientific education is required for some areas of the beverage industry. The issue of water quality is increasingly critical in this field. The Environmental Protection Agency is decreasing the levels of lead it deems tolerable in beverages and is also concerned about the by-products of disinfection: trihalomethanes and chloroforms. Issues involving quality control are likely to produce more jobs requiring technical skills. Additional business and management skills are needed for strategic planning to address these issues.

Exploring

If you are interested in a career in this field, begin exploring by doing some research. Read industry publications and visit their Web sites to learn about new trends, terminology, and important manufacturers. *Beverage World* magazine (http://www.beverageworld.com), *Beverage Digest* newsletter (http://www.beverage-digest.com), and *Tea & Coffee Trade Journal* (http://www.teaandcoffee.net) are good publications to take a look at. If there is a manufacturing plant in your area, try to get a summer or part-time job there. No matter what position you get, you'll have an inside look at the beverage industry. If there isn't a plant in your area, look for work in any setting offering interaction with the beverage industry, such as grocery stores, juice bars, coffee shops, and delivery services. These should also provide you with valuable work experience and give you the opportunity to learn what consumers like, how supplies are ordered and delivered, and what new products are available.

Employers

Employers in the beverage industry range from small bottling companies and importers of tea and coffee to international corporations such as Coca Cola, Pepsi Cola, Hills Brothers, Maxwell House,

Nestle, and Lipton Tea. Positions in route sales, advertising, and distributing are available in most cities and many smaller communities.

Starting Out

Positions in the beverage industry may be advertised in the employment section of local newspapers. Some workers belong to unions, and information about employment is available through union offices. Some positions may be listed with employment agencies. Applying to the human resources department of a local plant or company is a good way to find out about available jobs. Talking to a route salesman who may be visiting a local supermarket is another method of gaining information about companies. Large plants may offer tours to students and other individuals who may be seeking employment or who want to learn about an industry.

Advancement

With sufficient technical education and training, such as a degree in chemistry, workers can expect to advance to more technical positions in research and development or quality control. A college degree in business, management, or marketing as well as in-house training may lead to supervisory and management positions. Many years of experience in the industry may be necessary to reach higher administrative posts.

Earnings

Earnings for beverage industry workers vary based on their specific responsibilities, the size of their employer, the location, their union affiliation, their experience, and other such factors. Those in management, supervisory, research and development, or engineering positions naturally tend to have higher earnings. A sampling of job postings from Wade Palmer & Associates, a recruitment firm for food and beverage manufacturing professionals, provides salary ranges for a variety of positions. For example, the firm's Web site (http://www.job-recruiters.com) advertised quality control/assurance supervisor positions from around the country with a general salary range of $35,000 to $50,000 in 2002. Maintenance team leaders, responsible for overseeing the maintenance and repair of processing and packaging machinery, had a range of $40,000 to $60,000. Warehouse/distribution team leaders had a general range of $42,000 to $55,000. Of course, these earnings do not represent incomes for executives at the top of major corporations who may earn hundreds of thousands of dollars annually.

For workers on the production line, the U.S. Department of Labor provides earnings figures for a number of production occupations. The department reports, for example, that first-line supervisors/managers of production workers had mean annual earnings of $43,020 in 2000. Packaging and filling machine operators and tenders had a mean annual of $21,700, also in 2000. Ten percent of workers in this position made $13,250 or less annually, and 10 percent made $33,810 or more annually.

The National Soft Drink Association reports that the soft drink industry alone employs approximately 175,000 people across the country and that soft drink industry workers make a total of approximately $8 billion per year in salaries and wages.

Beverage industry workers generally have good benefits packages, including such things as health insurance, retirements plans or pensions, and paid vacation time.

Work Environment

According to the National Soft Drink Association, the modern bottling plant is a highly automated, sanitary environment. Highly sophisticated equipment handles the entire process, from the delicate mixing procedure to bottling to packaging. Voluntary compliance with HACCP, which became mandatory in the late 1990s, resulted in stricter standards of sanitation in the beverage industry. As with any plant in which technical equipment is used, there are always some safety risks. Eye-hand coordination plays an important role in this area.

Outlook

Beverage World magazine reports the global beverage marketplace is a $700 billion industry. Today, numerous mega-plants operate around the clock, seven days a week.

New drink products enter the market each year, and during the past decade, specialty companies, such as Starbucks Coffee and the many herbal tea manufacturers, have added millions of dollars and hundreds of jobs to the workplace. In addition to regular coffee, customers now can choose from espresso, café latte, hazelnut, mocha, and combinations of flavors. Engery drinks represent another growing area in the beverage industry. Figures from Beverage Marketing Corporation, a research group, revealed that dollar and volume growth in this segment was 110 percent during 2000 to 2001. In addition to growth from new products, carbonated soft drinks, the old stand-bys, continue to dominate the U.S. beverage industry. The average American drinks gallons and gallons of soft drinks every year. In fact, the Beverage Marketing Corporation reports that in 2001 the average amount was 55.4 gallons for every American. As long as people are thirsty, there should be steady job opportunities in this field.

For More Information

To learn more about the bottled water industry, water facts, and read news releases, visit the following Web site.
INTERNATIONAL BOTTLED WATER ASSOCIATION
1700 Diagonal Road, Suite 650
Alexandria, VA 22314
Tel: 703-683-5213
Web: http://www.bottledwater.org

For more information on education and other links, contact:
INTERNATIONAL SOCIETY OF BEVERAGE TECHNOLOGISTS
8110 South Suncoast Boulevard
Homosassa, FL 34446
Tel: 352-382-2008
Web: http://www.bevtech.org

For information on the soft drink market, contact:
NATIONAL SOFT DRINK ASSOCIATION
1101 16th Street, NW
Washington, DC 20036
Tel: 202-463-6732
Web: http://www.nsda.org

Brewers

Quick Facts

School Subjects
  Biology
  Chemistry
Personal Skills
  Following instructions
  Technical/scientific
Work Environment
  Primarily indoors
  Primarily one location
Minimum Education Level
  Some postsecondary training
Salary Range
  $20,000 to $34,090 to $65,000
Certification or Licensing
  Required for certain positions
Outlook
  About as fast as the average

Overview

Brewers oversee the production of many different styles of beer. They develop recipes that consist of various types and blends of the four basic ingredients: barley malt, hops, yeast, and water (and occasionally fruits, wheat, rice, and corn). Brewers add these ingredients into brewing vessels in accordance with the style of beer they are brewing and their own recipe. Brewers also tend to the brewing equipment. They monitor gauges and meters, as well as turn valves, open hatches, and occasionally stir.

History

The brewing of beer predates recorded history. Various beer-like drinks were discovered by many ancient civilizations including the Babylonians, Egyptians, Chinese, and Incas. Beer became especially prevalent in regions unsuitable for growing wine grapes. In the ninth century, Charlemagne (742-814) declared brewmasters among the artisans and laborers necessary for the prosperity of his kingdom. By the 11th century, modern beer, as we know it, was produced in the great breweries of Germany, and its commercial success grew significantly for the next several hundred years.

In 1609, American colonists placed want ads in a London newspaper asking for brewers to come to America. Many prominent Americans were concerned with the brewing of beer, including Samuel Adams (1722-1803), Thomas Jefferson (1743-1826), and George Washington (1732-99), who employed brewers at his

Mount Vernon estate. The great American brewing dynasties began with the German immigrants who arrived in the mid-1800s and settled in the Midwest. By the late 1800s there were more than 2,200 commercial breweries in the United States, the largest of them being Anheuser-Busch, Pabst, Miller, Stroh, and Schlitz.

The basic methods of brewing quality beers haven't changed much in the last 500 years. Although mass-market beers common in America today may skip steps, hasten others, or substitute ingredients for cost-cutting measures, the true science and art of craftbrewing has endured and resurged in the 1990s to produce fine American beers comparable to the best of the European market. Today's serious American brewer who is concerned with producing quality beers in the European or early American tradition is typically called a *craftbrewer*. Craftbrewers work at microbreweries, brewpubs, and contract brewers, known in the industry as third-tier brewers.

The Job

Brewers are concerned with all aspects of beer production, from selecting the exact blend and kind of flavoring hops, to the number of minutes the wort (liquid formed by soaking mash in hot water and fermenting it) boils. Beer styles and flavors are as multifarious as wine, and the craftbrewer can produce any number of beers for any occasion. Like great chefs, craftbrewers take particular pride in their recipes and enjoy presenting their "masterpieces" to others.

There are certain guidelines for each style of beer, but within those guidelines the brewer may experiment to create a truly unique flavor of a particular style. For example, a brewer who is making a pilsner must use bottom-fermenting, lager yeasts (as opposed to top-fermenting, ale yeasts), a light, dry barley malt (as opposed to a darker, roasted barley malt), and a specific few types of hops (most notably saaz, spalt, tettnanger, and hallertauer). With these basic guidelines observed, the brewer can experiment with such things as blending malts and hops, adding other flavors (such as honey, fruit, herbs, and spices), and varying boiling and lagering times.

The first step in brewing a batch of beer is for the brewer to decide what style he or she wants to brew. There are more than 50 styles of beer, many cousins of each other. Others are completely original and in their own class. All beers fall in one of two categories: they are either ales or lagers. Among the more common styles many

American craftbrewers are brewing today are ales (including pale ales, brown ales, and Scotch ales), pilsners, bocks, and double bocks, stouts, porters, and wheat beers (commonly know by their German name Weiss- or Weizenbier). With a particular beer style in mind, the brewer will seek the best ingredients to brew it.

The four basic ingredients of beer are malted barley, hops, yeast, and water. Some smaller breweries may use a malt extract. Some beers may call for wheat, rice, or corn in addition to barley. Malted barley not only contributes to the flavor and color of the beer, but more importantly, it provides food (fermentable sugars) for the yeast to produce alcohol. Brewers have a host of different types of yeast to choose from depending on the particular flavor they seek. There are two main varieties, top-fermenting ale yeasts and bottom-fermenting lager yeasts, and within each of these two varieties there are hundreds of strains, each imparting a different flavor to the beer. Hops come from a flower added to provide a contrasting bitterness and flavor to the sweet malt (called boiling hops), and to add a very important bouquet to the beer (called finishing, or aroma hops). Because beer is about 90 percent water, some brewers take the purity of their water very seriously. Water that has been treated with chlorine or that is rich in other minerals can impart unwanted flavors into a beer, which poses particular problems for brewers.

Malted barley must go through a mashing stage in the brewing process. Brewers grind the malted barley in specialized machines so that its husk is removed and the kernel broken. Next they add a precise amount of water and raise the temperature to between 150 and 160 degrees Fahrenheit to dissolve the natural sugars, starches, and enzymes of the barley. Brewers may vary the temperature and time of the mashing process to achieve a desired color or flavor. To complete the mashing process, the brewer strains out the barley grains. The remaining sweetened liquid, called malt extract, is now ready to become the wort.

Initially, wort is concentrated, unhopped beer. The brewer transfers the wort from the mashing vessel to a brewing kettle where boiling hops are added. This is usually just a matter of turning valves. Depending on the style of beer, the brewer will have selected a particular style or blend of hops. Some brewers use the actual hop leaf, others use a pelletized version. The hopped wort is boiled for an hour and a half to two and a half hours according to brewer preferences. After the wort has cooled to 50-60 degrees

Fahrenheit for lagers and 60-70 degrees Fahrenheit for ales, the hop leaves or pellet residue are removed in a process called sparging, and the wort is now ready for its most vital ingredient, yeast.

To ensure quality and consistency, many brewers culture their own yeast. Some smaller brewpubs or microbreweries use prepackaged yeast. Once the wort is cooled, the brewer transfers it to a starting tank where the yeast is added and the fermentation process begins. Depending on the style of beer and the desired results, the brewer will choose either an open or closed fermentation. Open fermentation is less common because it leaves the beer susceptible to airborne bacteria.

Most beers go through two basic fermentations; some beers require more. The initial contact of the wort and yeast spurs a fervent fermentation that produces alcohol and a foamy head called kraeusen. The brewer decides how long he or she wants this fermentation to last, generally between five and 14 days. After the desired time for the primary fermentation, the brewer transfers the beer to a lagering kettle (also called a conditioning kettle) where the beer is allowed to age. The fermentation continues but at a slower pace. The brewer must strictly regulate the temperature during the lagering time: 60-70 degrees Fahrenheit for ales, and 35-50 degrees Fahrenheit for lagers. After the desired aging or maturation of the beer, anywhere from two weeks to several months, the beer is again transferred to a storage tank where it is ready to be bottled. This step is necessary to leave any yeast or hops sediment behind so it is not present in the bottle or keg.

Brewers add carbonation to their beers either by injecting carbon dioxide into the storage tank just before it is to be bottled or kegged (this is typical of mass-produced beers) or, more common among craftbrewers, by adding a priming sugar, usually dry malt extract or corn sugar diluted in boiled water. If the brewer uses priming sugars, the beer must sit again for one to four weeks before it is ready to be served.

Brewing is both a creative and highly methodical craft requiring precise attention to detail. Brewers must monitor pH (acidity and alkalinity) levels in water and test water purity. They frequently use calculations to predict yields, efficiencies of processes, yeast maturation cycles, alcohol volume, bittering units, and many other factors. They study yeast physiology, metabolism, the biochemistry of fermentation and maturation, and the effects alternative brewing methods as well as bacteria, protozoa, and mold have on beer flavor and color. They constantly study methods of quality control and brewing efficiency.

Some craftbrewers at microbreweries may also help in bottling their beer. Workers at a brewpub (an establishment that is a combination brewery and restaurant) may stand behind the bar to pour drafts as well as work as waitstaff. At small breweries, brewers frequently sterilize their tanks, kettles, hoses, and other brewing equipment. Brewers who have the right resources and live in the right environment may grow, harvest, and store their own hops. Many craftbrewers are responsible for marketing their beer or designing logos. Some co-manage the brewpub or microbrewery. But a brewer's primary duty is always to brew beer, to experiment and come up with new recipes, and to seek out the right ingredients for the particular style of beer that is being brewed.

Requirements

HIGH SCHOOL

In today's competitive job market, aspiring brewers need a high school degree to land a job with growth possibilities, a good salary, and challenges, including positions in the craftbrewing industry.

High school classes in biology, chemistry, and mathematics will be particularly useful if you are interested in becoming a brewer. Classes in biochemistry and microbiology will prepare you for the more specialized aspects of brewing that serious craftbrewers must master. A background in science and mathematics is needed for brewers to perform basic brewing and engineering calculations and to follow technical discussions on brewing topics. Classes in home economics or family and consumer science can teach you basic kitchen skills, common units of cooking measurement, and the organizational skills you need to prepare and complete complex recipes. If you are interested in running your own microbrewery, be sure to take business, accounting, and computer science classes to help you prepare for managing a business.

POSTSECONDARY TRAINING

Employers today prefer to hire only brewers who have completed some kind of formal training program in brewing sciences, or who have had extensive apprenticeship training at another brewery. The following three institutions are the most prominent U.S. schools offering programs on brewing sciences and the business of brewing. The Siebel Institute of Technology & World Brewing Academy is located in Chicago, Illinois, with a partner campus in Munich, Germany. The Siebel Institute offers courses on specific topics, such as brewing microbiology, and the World Brewing Academy offers a diploma program that lasts 12 weeks and involves work done in Chicago and Munich. The American Brewers Guild is located in Woodland, California. The Craft Brewers Apprenticeship Program of the American Brewers Guild lasts 27 weeks and combines classroom work with hands-on experience. Graduates receive a diploma and job placement assistance. The University Extension, University of California, Davis, Professional Brewing Programs offers certificate options as well as a master brewers program. Although a college degree is not required for admission to the professional brewing programs, you will need to have completed college coursework in the following areas: biological sciences (biology, biochemistry, microbiology), chemistry, physics, mathematics (pre-calculus), and engineering.

It is highly recommended that you complete an organized course of study through one of these programs. Students who learn at a brewing sciences school will have a particular advantage in landing a job as a brewer because employers know graduates have received training in the many highly technical aspects of brewing. Topics covered usually include brewing raw materials, brewhouse theory and practice, fermentation, storage and finishing, packaging and engineering topics, quality control, microbiology laboratory, and sensory evaluation.

CERTIFICATION OR LICENSING
Breweries of any size must be licensed both by the state in which they are located and the Bureau of Alcohol, Tobacco, and Firearms, which is part of the U.S. Treasury Department. Owners of breweries are responsible for obtaining and maintaining these licenses.

OTHER REQUIREMENTS
Brewers must have an avid appreciation for beer and an excellent sense of taste. They must be able to detect all of a particular beer's

subtleties and nuances through taste and aroma. They should also be able to distinguish between styles of beer.

Brewers need good organizational and problem-solving skills as well as creativity. If a batch of beer turns out bad, the brewer must be able, through tests or experience, to pinpoint what went wrong and why. Beer takes time to brew. While the process can be hastened, craftbrewers should have the patience to allow beer to brew in its natural time. Brewers must be able to follow recipes and procedures closely, but they must also know when and how to go beyond a recipe's direction, or when to vary a procedure to achieve a desired result. Brewers must be 21 or older.

Exploring

Most breweries, whether a microbrewery, a brewpub, or one of the major mass-production breweries, offer tours of their facilities. This is an excellent opportunity to learn what actually goes on in a brewery, to see the brewing equipment and the raw ingredients, and to ask questions. Those 21 and older will be able to sample the various styles of beer at the brewery and ask questions of the masterbrewer.

Homebrewing is a popular trend that has been growing rapidly for the past decade. Those 21 and over can learn firsthand how to brew small batches of beer at home. The equipment and ingredients needed to begin brewing can be found at some larger liquor stores or through mail order. There are numerous books and magazines available on the subject. *Zymurgy*, the American Homebrewers Association's magazine, focuses on homebrewing issues, and The New Brewer, the Institute for Brewing Studies' magazine, covers topics of interest to micro- and pubbrewers. Sample articles as well as information on other publications can be found at the Association of Brewers' Web site, http://www.beer-town.org. Most brewers began their experience with brewing by brewing first at home. So you're not of legal drinking age yet? Don't worry, you can still learn some of the basic skills of a brewer by making nonalcoholic carbonated drinks, such as sodas. Articles on this topic are frequently found in beer magazines because so much of the same equipment is used to make each.

Some breweries have part-time jobs available to students. They usually entail sanitizing the brewing equipment after a batch has been made or transporting heavy bags of ingredients. This is an excellent opportunity to learn how the brewing machines work, to get to know the various types of ingredients, and to see the types of challenges and pressures brewers face.

Starting Out

The best career path for an aspiring craftbrewer is to begin as a homebrewer, learning the basic methods and science of brewing and possibly developing a personal style. Until recently, many brewers still learned the trade through hands-on experience as an apprentice at a microbrewery or brewpub. Although this is still an option, an increasing number of brewers are completing formal postsecondary training, making the market more competitive. Due to the recent renaissance in American brewing, employers are looking to hire highly qualified brewers who will not require years of on-the-job-training but can immediately begin producing quality beers. An added benefit of getting postsecondary training is the job placement assistance any respected school provides to its graduates.

Currently, however, there are not enough trained craftbrewers to fill the demand, so many breweries still employ apprentices who have some experience in brewing—generally as homebrewers. Apprentices may spend several years learning the craft from a masterbrewer. They usually begin by sanitizing brewing vessels, preparing ingredients for the masterbrewer, and doing some administrative work, all the while taking notes and observing brewing techniques.

Breweries looking for trained craftbrewers often post job openings at brewing schools or advertise in trade magazines or local papers. There are many beer festivals and homebrewing contests where breweries—particularly new breweries—seek out the brewers of winning beers and offer them work.

Advancement

Brewers advance as the popularity of their beer increases and continual sales are made. Most microbreweries and brewpubs are led by the so-called *masterbrewer* (often the one who developed the recipe), and depending on the size of the brewery, there may be *general brewers* who help in the brewing process. After demonstrating resourcefulness in technique, or after developing a successful beer recipe on their own, these general brewers may advance to masterbrewer at the brewery where they work, or they may transfer to become masterbrewer at a different brewery. Their work will still be the same, but as masterbrewer, they will be able to relegate work to others and earn a larger salary. After an approximate two-year period of learning the brewing process, an apprentice will advance to become a general brewer or even masterbrewer.

Most brewers are content to remain masterbrewer of a microbrewery or brewpub, but some may advance to management positions if the opportunity arises. *Brewery managers* are responsible for the day-to-day operations of a brewery, including managing finances, marketing, and hiring employees. Many microbreweries are operated by a small staff, and advancement for brewers may simply mean increasing brewery output and doing good business.

Earnings

Salaries for those in the brewing business vary considerably based on several factors, including the size of the brewery, its location, the popularity of its beer, and the length of time the brewery has been in business. Brewers running their own microbreweries or brewpubs, like any small business owner, may have very low take-home wages for several years as the business becomes established. According to the Economic Research Institute, masterbrewers with five years of experience average $46,170, with top earnings at $57,250 per year. The institute also reports that those with 10 years of experience average $53,098 annually, and top earnings were $65,000. According to the U.S. Department of Labor, the average hourly pay for production workers throughout the beverage industry was $16.39 in 2000. This hourly wage translates into a yearly income of approximately $34,090 for full-time work.

Brewers running their own businesses must pay for benefits (health insurance, retirement plans, etc.) themselves. Brewers employed by breweries can generally expect health insurance and paid vacation time. Other benefits may include dental and eye care, life and disability insurance, and a pension plan. Many employers will pay for all or part of a brewer's training. A brewer's salary can increase by yearly bonuses or profit sharing if the brewery does well in the course of a year. Most brewers confess that the greatest benefit of their job is free beer.

Work Environment

Most of a brewer's time is spent in the brewery preparing the next batch of beer. At many small microbreweries and brewpubs, brewers are responsible for all of the brewery operations. Before preparing a batch of beer, they use hoses and brushes with a sanitizing solution and clean all of the kettles. Since sanitization is a very crucial part of brewing, this must be a very thorough job and is, therefore, often strenuous. Temperatures in breweries are strictly controlled, in some cases to as low as 40 degrees Fahrenheit.

The size of the brewery dictates a craftbrewer's working hours. A small brewery can only produce a limited amount of beer at one time. Brewers may have days when they are not brewing at all. Instead they may perform maintenance on equipment, prepare yeast cultures, or even grow and harvest hops. Many brewers experiment with new styles of beer by brewing small five-gallon batches. Brewers spend a lot of time tasting many different styles and brands of beers to determine what qualities make the beer good and what qualities make it bad, so that they can improve their own beer. Brewers, especially those at small breweries, may work odd hours (until very late at night or very early in the morning) in order to move the brew from one stage in the brewing process to another. Brewers usually work about 40 hours a week. Those who own breweries or brewpubs, however, often work much longer hours than this to complete all the management tasks required of a business.

Outlook

America is currently in the midst of a beer renaissance. An increasing number of alcoholic beverage drinkers have discovered that beer can be as complex as wine and equally enjoyable. Clearly, taste preferences have changed for a large segment of the beer-drinking population from the bland, almost watery styles of the major beer manufacturers to a more complex, hearty style of the craftbeer producers. Even the major brewers like Miller, Anheuser Busch, and Coors have acknowledged the craftbrewing trend by introducing their own premium-style beers—and to great success.

Although craftbrewing accounts for only a small percentage (about 3 percent) of the U.S. beer market, it is a growing segment of the beer industry. According to the Institute for Brewing

Studies, there are now more than 1,450 microbreweries, brewpubs, and regional specialty breweries operating across the country. The craftbrewing industry's annual dollar volume was approximately $3.2 billion in 2000. As people have become accustomed to the availability of unique tasting beers, they have created a growing market for these products.

Like any small business, just-opened brewpubs and microbreweries will succeed or fail on an individual basis. The craftbrewing industry itself, however, is here to stay. A strong demand for excellent brewers exists, and those with training should have the best opportunities.

For More Information

To learn about the Craftbrewers Apprenticeship Program, contact:
AMERICAN BREWERS GUILD
908 Ross Drive
Woodland, CA 95776
Email: abg@abgbrew.com
Web: http://www.abgbrew.com

For industry statistics, information on professional brewing and homebrewing, and related publications, contact:
ASSOCIATION OF BREWERS
736 Pearl Street
Boulder, CO 80302
Tel: 303-447-0816
Web: http://www.beertown.org

For more information about the Professional Brewing Programs offered through the University Extension, University of California, Davis, contact:
UNIVERSITY EXTENSION
1333 Research Park Drive
Davis, CA 95616
Tel: 800-752-0881
Web: http://universityextension.ucdavis.edu/brewing

Canning and Preserving Industry Workers

Overview

Canning and preserving industry workers monitor equipment and perform routine tasks in food-processing plants that can, preserve, and quick-freeze such foods as vegetables, fruits, frozen dinners, jams, jellies, preserves, pickles, and soups. They also process and preserve seafood, including shrimp, oysters, crabs, clams, and fish.

History

As soon as people learned to grow and harvest food, they faced the problem of keeping that food from spoiling so that it could last until the next harvest. Centuries ago, people discovered that salting, drying, and pickling could preserve many meats, fruits, and vegetables. In colonial America, most of this preserving was done in the home. Families grew their own fruits and vegetables and preserved them to make them last through the winter months.

In 1795, the French government sought better ways to feed its army, especially ways to keep foods from spoiling, and offered a prize to anyone who could develop a method of keeping foods edible and portable for a long period of time. Nicolas Appert, a chef in Paris, took up the challenge and developed the first canning process. In 1810, Appert developed a system of bottling foods, corking the bottles and holding the corks in place with wire, and then heating the bottles. At the same time in England, the first tin-coated metal cans were developed, and these were soon applied to food preservation using Appert's method. Appert's process became known as *canning*.

Since the Industrial Revolution, and especially in the 20th century, advances in refrigeration and sanitation and new applications of many industrial processes of food preparation have almost completely transferred the business of preserving food to large factories. Freezing was applied to food preservation in the 1920s, and ways were sought to freeze foods as quickly as possible, thereby preserving not only their flavor but also their nutritional value. Scientists also discovered that certain chemicals could preserve food by killing off microorganisms or preventing them from reproducing. Later, irradiation became another controversial method of food preservation. Factory-preserved fruits, fish, soup, and vegetables are found in almost every refrigerator and kitchen cupboard in the nation. Canning and preservation techniques have made it possible for people to enjoy foods from all over the world, and at all times of the year.

For much of the past century, canning and preserving were labor-intensive; that is, they required many people to manually perform the various steps of processing, preserving, and packaging foods. In recent years, automated machinery and equipment, which are often computer-controlled, have greatly increased the quantity of foods that can be processed and have made it possible for many foods to be processed, canned, and preserved without ever being touched by human hands.

The Job

In order to operate successfully, a food-processing plant must have plenty of the foodstuff it processes. Therefore, many workers in the canning and preserving industry work outside processing plants arranging for this supply of raw materials. *Field contractors* negotiate with farmers to grow certain kinds of food crops for processing. They work with farmers to decide what to plant, how to grow the crop, and when to harvest it. They reach agreements concerning price, the quantity that will be delivered, and the quality standards that the crop must meet. *Purchasing agents* purchase raw materials and other goods for processing.

When unprocessed food arrives at the factory, *graders,* including *fruit-buying graders,* examine produce and record its quality, or grade, and mark it for separation by class, size, color, and condition.

Wharf laborers unload catches of fish for processing from the wharf and transport the fish to the processing plant's storage area. *Fish-bin tenders* sort fish according to species and size.

At the plant, the *plant superintendent* coordinates processing activities to coincide with crop harvesting. The *plant manager* hires workers, contacts buyers, and coordinates maintenance and operation of plant machinery.

Most processing of food is done with automatic machines. *Dumping-machine operators* run machines that grip, tilt, and dump boxes of produce onto conveyor belts leading to washing vats. Workers then wash food and inspect the produce, removing damaged or spoiled items before they can be processed. *Sieve-grader tenders* and *sorting-machine operators* tend machines that sort vegetables, shrimp, and pickles according to size.

Plants that process fish and shellfish may kill, shell, and clean the fish before processing. *Crab butchers* butcher live crabs before canning. *Fish cleaners* and *fish-cleaning-machine operators* scale, slice open, and eviscerate fish. Using a shucking knife, *shellfish shuckers* pry open oyster, clam, and scallop shells and remove the meat. Shrimp are often shelled by machines that are operated by workers who must make adjustments according to the size of the shrimp. Later *separator operators* remove any sand or remaining shell particles from shellfish meats using water or air-agitating machines. Alternatively, bone pickers look for shell particles by placing shellfish meats under ultraviolet light and picking shell bits out by hand. Other workers operate machines that wash, steam, brine, and peel shellfish.

Often only one part of a fruit or vegetable is wanted for processing. Many workers operate machines that peel or extract the desired parts from produce. *Finisher operators* run machines that remove the skin and seeds from tomatoes, leaving pulp that is used in sauces and catsup. *Lye-peel operators* run machines that use lye and water to remove skins of fruits and vegetables. *Fruit-press operators* run power presses to extract juice from fruit for flavorings and syrup, and *extractor-machine operators* extract juice from citrus fruits.

Food must often be cut into pieces of the proper size and shape for preserving. *Meat blenders* grind meat for use in baby food. Many workers operate machines that cut or chop produce, and *fish butchers* and *fish choppers* cut fish into pieces and lengths for freezing or canning.

Next, foods are cooked. Some are cooked before and others after they are sealed in packages. Many vegetables are blanched (scalded with hot water or steam) before packaging, by *blanching-machine operators. Kettle cooks* and *kettle cook helpers* cook other fish, fruits, and vegetables in large kettles before packaging. These workers must measure and load water and uncooked food into the kettles; stir, monitor, and test foods as they cook; and remove cooked food from the kettles. Other workers cook fish, meat, and vegetables by deep-frying before freezing. *Vacuum-kettle cooks* vacuum-cook fruits and berries for jam and jelly.

Other foods, including many vegetables, are processed after they have been sealed in cans. *Packers* fill cans or jars with food to specified volume and weight. Other workers operate closing machines to put an airtight seal on the containers. Containers are then taken to retort chambers. Retorts are like huge steam pressure cookers, and they can heat food containers to temperatures between 240 degrees Fahrenheit and 260 degrees Fahrenheit. *Retort operators* load, start, and stop these machines according to specifications. Food must then be quickly cooled to stop cooking. *Pasteurizers* kill bacteria in bottles, canned foods, and beverages using a hot water spray or steam.

Some food is preserved using brine, a concentrated solution of salt in water that acts as a preservative. *Brine makers* measure ingredients for the solution and boil it in a steam cooker for a specified amount of time. They test the solution's salinity with a hydrometer and pump it to a processing vat. They may also operate the vats and empty and clean them when necessary. *Picklers* mix ingredients for pickling vegetables, fruits, fish, and meat and soak these foods for a specified period of time. *Briners* immerse fresh fish fillets in brine to condition them for freezing.

Some food is prepared for canning by removing moisture, and some fish is smoked to preserve it. *Fish smokers* put salt-cured fish on racks in a smoke chamber and turn a valve to admit smoke into the chamber.

Many foods are frozen fresh or after blanching. *Freezing-room workers* move racks of packaged food in and out of freezing rooms. They keep track of the amount of time food has been in the freezing room and remove the food when it is sufficiently frozen to transport to a warehouse or onto delivery trucks. *Freezer-tunnel operators* quick-freeze foods.

Other foods, especially fruits, are preserved by drying. *Dehydrator tenders* bleach and dehydrate fruit, while other workers dry eggs, milk, and potatoes.

Once food has been canned, it is labeled, tested, and inspected. *Vacuum testers* tap can lids to make sure they are vacuum sealed. *Can inspectors* check seams of closed food and beverage cans by cutting and taking measurements of seams of sample cans. *X-ray inspectors* X-ray jars of baby food to ensure they contain no foreign materials.

Other workers clean cooking kettles and other equipment. *Production helpers* perform a variety of unskilled tasks in canning and preserving plants. Workers may also be designated according to the food they prepare: steak sauce makers, mincemeat makers, relish blenders, and horseradish makers, for example.

Requirements

HIGH SCHOOL
There are no minimum educational requirements for many food-processing jobs, although most employers prefer to hire high school graduates; a high school diploma is essential for those seeking advancement. Beginners seldom need previous experience, and usually they can learn their jobs quickly. Generally there is up to one month of on-the-job training.

POSTSECONDARY TRAINING
Many plants provide orientation sessions for new workers and programs on safety and sanitation. For those who aspire to management positions, a college degree is recommended, with studies in accounting, management, and other business courses as well as chemistry.

CERTIFICATION OR LICENSING

Some skilled and technical staff in plants in some states must be licensed. Retort room supervisors are required by the Food and Drug Administration to attend an instructional program in retort operation.

OTHER REQUIREMENTS

Manual dexterity is a useful characteristic for many workers in the canning and preserving industry, as are reliability and willingness to learn.

Exploring

Students may arrange to tour a food-processing plant in their area. Such a visit can be a good way to get a general overview of the jobs in the plant. Talking to people employed in different jobs in canning or preserving plants is another good way to learn something about the field. Because some food-processing work is seasonal, part-time job opportunities for students may be limited. However, temporary employment, such as during summer harvest season, may be possible.

Employers

Canning and preserving work is available in a variety of manufacturing plants. The type of products to be canned or preserved depends in part on what grows, grazes, or swims in a particular area. Coastal areas may have fish-processing plants, while the Midwest has more meat products. Farm regions may have plants that process products grown nearby. However, because of refrigeration and other technology, other factors, such as shipping routes and access to workers, may determine where plants are located. Manufacturers may be small companies or multinational organizations.

Starting Out

Applying to canneries, freezing plants, and other food-processing plants is the most direct method of finding work in this area. Employers may advertise openings in newspaper want ads or with the state employment service. Those interested in processing fish and seafood may find year-round work in canneries and processing ships in Alaska or follow the fishing seasons along the west and east coasts.

Advancement

Workers with a high school education start out as sorters or helpers or in similar unskilled positions. Advancement opportunities from these positions are limited. In time, some workers can move into field contractor positions. For those interested in more advanced positions, such as food technologists and food scientists, a college degree in a related course of study is required.

Earnings

Although some products can be processed at any time during the year, the level of activity in many food-processing plants varies with the season, and earnings of workers vary accordingly. Larger plants overcome the seasonality of their food products by maintaining large inventories of raw foodstuffs, and workers for these plants generally work full-time throughout the year. Earnings for workers in the canning and preserving industry vary widely. Many positions, especially at the entry level, pay little more than the minimum wage. The following averages show the variety of earnings possible in this industry. According to the U.S. Department of Labor, those processing workers working in preserving fruits and vegetables earned an average of $12.11 per hour in 2000 (approximately $25,190 a year for full-time work). Inspectors, testers, and sorters in food processing earned $10.92 per hour (approximately $22,715 annually). Food processing packaging workers made an average of $10.51 per hour (about $21,860 per year), and those operating food cooking machines had an hourly average of $10.47 (approximately $21,780 annually). Meat and fish cutters and trimmers averaged $7.99 per hour (approximately $16,620 per year). Those in supervisory positions, such as plant managers, have higher earnings. According to the U.S. Department of Labor, the middle 50 percent of industrial production managers, including those working in food products, had annual earnings ranging from $46,290 to $81,930.

Generally, seasonal workers earn an hourly wage; some, particularly those working on processing ships or for canneries in Alaska, also receive board and lodging. Benefits vary from company to company.

Work Environment

Canning and preserving plants are located in many parts of the country. Most plants are located close to the supply source and are staffed by local people who sometimes hold other jobs as well. During harvest season, plants may operate 24 hours a day, with three work shifts.

In plants where food is frozen, some workers spend considerable time in temperatures that are well below freezing. These workers wear special clothing and take periodic warm-up breaks during the day. Canneries, on the other hand, may be damp, noisy, and odorous. In some jobs, workers need to be on their feet for long periods, and often the tasks are very repetitive.

Outlook

The use of automated equipment and computer technology throughout the food-processing industry means that fewer people will be needed to process, preserve, and can foods. Wherever it is efficient and economical, machines will take over the tasks that people have been doing. Therefore, the U.S. Department of Labor predicts a decline in overall employment in the industry through 2010. Researchers and technical workers with specialized expertise and college-level training will have the best employment opportunities.

In some kinds of food processing, such as the fish canneries in Alaska, employment levels are related to weather and other natural factors that vary from year to year.

For More Information

For facts, statistics, and news, contact:
AMERICAN FROZEN FOOD INSTITUTE
2000 Corporate Ridge, Suite 1000
McLean, VA 22102
Tel: 703-821-0770
Email: info@affi.com
Web: http://www.affi.com

For information on careers, education, scholarships, and student memberships, contact:
INSTITUTE OF FOOD TECHNOLOGISTS
221 North LaSalle Street, Suite 300
Chicago, IL 60601-1291
Tel: 312-782-8424
Email: info@ift.org
Web: http://www.ift.org

For information on the industry and safety issues, contact:
NATIONAL FOOD PROCESSORS ASSOCIATION
1350 I Street, NW, Suite 300
Washington, DC 20005
Tel: 202-639-5900
Email: nfpa@nfpa-food.org
Web: http://www.nfpa-food.org

Caterers

Quick Facts

School Subjects
Business
Family and consumer science

Personal Skills
Artistic
Helping/teaching

Work Environment
Primarily indoors
Primarily multiple locations

Minimum Education Level
Some postsecondary training

Salary Range
$15,000 to $35,000 to $75,000+

Certification or Licensing
Voluntary (certification)
Required by certain states
(licensing)

Outlook
About as fast as the average

Overview

Caterers plan, coordinate, and supervise food service at parties and at other social functions. Working with their clients, they purchase appropriate supplies, plan menus, supervise food preparation, direct serving of food and refreshments, and ensure the overall smooth functioning of the event. As entrepreneurs, they are also responsible for budgeting, bookkeeping, and other administrative tasks.

History

Catering is part of the food service industry and has been around for as long as there have been restaurants. Once viewed as a service available only to the very wealthy, who used caterers to supplement their own hired staff for grand occasions, catering today is used by many people for many different types of gatherings.

The Job

A caterer is a chef, purchasing agent, personnel director, and accountant. Often a caterer will also play the role of host, allowing clients to enjoy their own party. A caterer's responsibilities vary, depending on the size of the catering firm and the specific needs of individual clients. While preparing quality food is a concern no matter what the size of the party, larger events require far more planning and coordination. For example, a large catering firm may organize and plan a formal event for a thousand people, including planning and preparing a seven-course meal, decorating the hall with flowers and wall hangings, employing 20 or more wait staff to serve food, and arranging the entertainment. The catering firm will also set up the tables and chairs and provide the necessary linen, silverware, and dishes. A catering company may organize 50 or so such events a month or only several a year. A smaller catering organization may concentrate on simpler events, such as preparing food for an informal buffet for 15 people.

Caterers service not only individual clients but also industrial clients. A caterer may supervise a company cafeteria or plan food service for an airline or cruise ship. Such caterers often take over full-time supervision of food operations, including ordering food and other supplies, supervising personnel and food preparation, and overseeing the maintenance of equipment.

Caterers need to be flexible in their approach to food preparation, that is, able to prepare food both on- and off-premises, as required by logistical considerations and the wishes of the client. For example, if the caterer is handling a large banquet in a hotel or other location, he or she will usually prepare the food on-premises, using kitchen and storage facilities as needed. The caterer might also work in a client's kitchen for an event in a private home. In both cases, the caterer must visit the site of the function well before the actual event to determine how and where the food will be prepared. Caterers may also prepare food off-premises, working either in their own kitchens or in a mobile kitchen.

Working with the client is obviously a very important aspect of the caterer's job. Clients always want their affairs to be extra special, and the caterer's ability to present such items as a uniquely shaped wedding cake or to provide beautiful decorations will enhance the ambiance and contribute to customer satisfaction. The caterer and the client work together to establish a budget, develop a menu, and determine the desired atmosphere. Many caterers have their own special recipes, and they are always on the lookout for quality fruits, vegetables, and meats. Caterers should have an eye for detail and be able to make fancy hors d'oeuvres and eye-catching fruit and vegetable displays.

Although caterers can usually prepare a variety of dishes, they may have a specialty, such as Cajun or Italian cuisine. Caterers may also have a special serving style, such as serving food in

Renaissance period dress, that sets them apart from other caterers. Developing a reputation by specializing in a certain area is an especially effective marketing technique.

The caterer is a coordinator who works with suppliers, food servers, and the client to ensure that an event comes off as planned. The caterer must be in frequent contact with all parties involved in the affair, making sure, for example, that the food is delivered on time, the flowers are fresh, and the entertainment shows up and performs as promised.

Good management skills are extremely important. The caterer must know how much food and other supplies to order, what equipment will be needed, how many staff to hire, and how to coordinate various activities to ensure a smooth-running event. Purchasing the proper supplies entails knowledge of a variety of food products, their suppliers, and the contacts needed to get the right product at the best possible price.

Caterers working in a large operation may appoint a manager to oversee an event. The manager will take care of the ordering, planning, and supervising responsibilities and may even work with the client.

As entrepreneurs, caterers have many important day-to-day administrative responsibilities, such as overseeing the budgeting and bookkeeping of the operation. They must make sure that the business continues to make a profit while keeping its prices competitive. Additionally, caterers must know how to figure costs and other budgetary considerations, plan inventories, buy food, and ensure compliance with health regulations.

Caterer helpers may prepare and serve hors d'oeuvres and other food and refreshments at social functions under the supervision of the head caterer. They also help arrange tables and decorations and then assist in the cleanup.

Requirements

HIGH SCHOOL
Does working as a caterer sound interesting to you? If so, you should take home economics or family and consumer science classes in high school. Any class that will teach you about food preparation, presentation, and nutrition will be valuable. Since

caterers run their own businesses you should also take math, accounting and bookkeeping, and business classes to prepare for dealing with budgets, record keeping, and management. Like so many small business owners today, most caterers will use computers for such things as planning schedules, keeping addresses, and updating accounts, so be sure to take computer classes. English classes will help you to hone your communication skills, which will be essential when you deal with customers. Finally, round out your education by taking health and science classes, which will give you an added understanding of nutrition, how the body works, and how to prevent food contamination.

POSTSECONDARY TRAINING
The best way to enter the catering industry is through a formal training program. One way of obtaining this education is to attend a vocational or community college with an appropriate program. Many of these schools and colleges offer professional training in food science, food preparation, and catering. Often these programs will provide opportunities for students to work in apprentice positions to gain hands-on experience.

As the catering field has grown more competitive, many successful caterers are now choosing to get a college degree in business administration, family and consumer science (home economics), nutrition, or a related field. If you decide to get a four-year college degree, make sure your coursework includes subjects in nutrition, health, and business management, regardless of your major. A number of colleges and universities also offer assistance to their students in finding apprenticeships. The Foundation of the National Association of Catering Executives (NACE) provides information on universities and colleges offering programs relevant to those interested in the catering profession.

CERTIFICATION OR LICENSING
As a measure of professional status, many caterers become certified through NACE. To qualify for this certification, called the Certified Professional Catering Executive (CPCE), caterers must meet certain educational and professional requirements as well as pass a written examination. To keep their certification current, caterers must also fulfill requirements such as completing continuing education courses and attending professional conferences. The

International Food Service Executives Association also offers the Certified Food Executive (CFE) and the Certified Food Manager (CFM) designations. Applications are available online; see the Web site listed at the end of the article for more information.

Most states require caterers to be licensed, and inspectors may make periodic visits to catering operations to ensure that local health and safety regulations are being maintained in food preparation, handling, and storage.

OTHER REQUIREMENTS

Foods go in and out of fashion, new technologies develop, and our understanding of nutrition and health is always growing. The successful caterer will want to keep up with all these new developments in the field. Because caterers run their own businesses, they should be organized, able to work on tight schedules, and conscientious about keeping accurate records. Caterers should enjoy working with people and be able to arrange food in an appealing manner.

Exploring

One relatively simple way for you to begin exploring your interest in catering is to do some cooking at home. Make dinner for your family once a week or bake cookies for your friends. If people enjoy your creations, you may be able to offer catering services to them when they have parties.

Another great way to explore food service is through service work. Volunteering in the kitchen of a local homeless shelter where you can help prepare meals for large numbers of people can provide a great experience, both for your professional ambitions and for humanitarian reasons.

Finally, get part-time or summer work at a local restaurant. Even if you end up working at an ice cream parlor when what you really want to do is cater eight-course meals, you'll still gain valuable experience working with food, money, and customers.

Employers

Most caterers own their own businesses and are, therefore, self-employed. Caterers, however, do have many different types of clients. Individuals may need catering services for a party or special family celebration. Industrial clients, such as company cafeterias, airlines, country clubs, schools, banquet halls, cruise ships, and hotels, may require catering services on a large scale or at regular intervals.

Starting Out

Some caterers enter the profession as a matter of chance after helping a friend or relative prepare a large banquet or volunteering to coordinate a group function. Most caterers, however, begin their careers after graduating from college with a degree in a program such as home economics or finishing a culinary training program at a vocational school or community college.

Qualified people may begin work as a manager for a large catering firm or as a manager for a hotel or country club or banquet service. An individual will most likely start a catering business only with extensive experience and sufficient finances to purchase equipment and cover other start-up costs.

Advancement

The success of a caterer depends on the quality of work and a good reputation. Well-known caterers can expand their businesses from a small business to a larger operation. Caterers who work out of their own home kitchens may get an office or relocate to another area in order to take advantage of better catering opportunities. Sometimes successful caterers use their skills and reputations to secure full-time positions in large hotels or restaurants as *banquet coordinators.* Independent caterers may also secure contracts with industrial clients, such as airlines, hospitals, schools, and corporations, to staff their cafeterias or supply food and beverages. They may also be employed by such companies to manage their food operations.

Earnings

Earnings vary widely, depending on the size and location of the catering operation and the skill and motivation of the individual entrepreneur. Many caterers charge according to the number of guests attending a function. In many cases, the larger the event, the larger the profit. Earnings are also influenced by whether a caterer works full-time or only part-time. Even very successful caterers often work part-time, working another job either because they enjoy it or to protect themselves against a possible downturn in the economy.

Full-time caterers can earn between $15,000 and $60,000 per year, depending on skill, reputation, and experience. An extremely successful caterer can easily earn more than $75,000 annually. A part-time caterer may earn $7,000 to $15,000 per year, subject to the same variables as the full-time caterer. Because most caterers are self-employed, vacations and other benefits are usually not part of the wage structure.

According to the U.S. Department of Labor, a caterer who is employed as a manager for a company cafeteria or other industrial client may earn between $19,000 and $50,000 per year, with vacation, health insurance, and other benefits usually included.

Work Environment

A caterer often works long hours planning and preparing for an event, and the day of the event might easily be a 14-hour workday, from setup to cleanup. Caterers often spend long hours on their feet, and although the work can be physically and mentally demanding, they usually enjoy a great deal of work flexibility. As entrepreneurs, they can usually take time off when necessary. Caterers often work more than 60 hours a week during busy seasons, with most of the work on weekends and evenings, when events tend to be scheduled.

There is a lot of variety in the type of work a caterer does. The caterer must work closely with a variety of clients and be able to adapt to last minute changes. Caterers must be able to plan ahead, work gracefully under pressure, and have the ability to adapt to last minute mishaps. Attention to detail is critical, as is the ability to work long hours under demanding situations. They must be able to direct a large staff of kitchen workers and waitpersons and be able to interact well with clients, guests, and employees.

Outlook

The U.S. Department of Labor projects that employment opportunities in food service should continue to grow at an average rate through 2010. Opportunities will be good for individuals who handle special events, such as weddings, bar and bat mitzvahs, and other festive occasions less affected by downswings in the economy. On the other hand, events such as business functions may offer less catering opportunities during times of recession and cutbacks.

Competition is keen as many hotels and restaurants branch out to offer catering services. However, despite competition and fluctuating economic conditions, highly skilled and motivated caterers should be in demand throughout the country, especially in and around large metropolitan areas.

For More Information

For information on scholarships, student branches, certification, and industry news, contact:
INTERNATIONAL FOOD SERVICE EXECUTIVES ASSOCIATION
15724 Edgewood Street
Livonia, MI 48154-2312
Email: hq@ifsea.org
Web: http://www.ifsea.org

For information on certification programs and catering publications, contact:
NATIONAL ASSOCIATION OF CATERING EXECUTIVES
5565 Sterrett Place, Suite 328
Columbia, MD 21044
Tel: 410-997-9055
Web: http://www.nace.net

For more information on programs and chapters, contact:
NATIONAL 4-H COUNCIL
7100 Connecticut Avenue
Chevy Chase, MD 20815
Tel: 301-961-2800
Web: http://www.fourhcouncil.edu

Confectionery Industry Workers

Quick Facts

School Subjects
  Biology
  Chemistry
  Family and consumer science
Personal Skills
  Following instructions
  Technical/scientific
Work Environment
  Primarily indoors
  Primarily one location
Minimum Education Level
  High school diploma
Salary Range
  $10,700 to $26,105 to $30,890+
Certification or Licensing
  None available
Outlook
  Decline

Overview

Confectionery industry workers manufacture and package sweets, including bonbons, hard and soft candy, stuffed dates, popcorn balls, and many other types of confections. There are 48,000 confectionery industry workers in the United States.

History

Confections have been made since ancient times. The word "sugar" may have come from Sanskrit, the ancient language of India; the word "candy" came from the Persian "qand" which means sugar. Cane sugar has been used in the making of sweets since ancient times in the Far East. Its use gradually spread west; by the 1600s, the making of confections based on sugar was considered an art form through much of Europe. One of the world's most popular confections, chocolate, has its origins in Central and South America, where the cacao bean, from which chocolate is made, has been cultivated for thousands of years. Spanish explorers imported the bean to West Africa, where most of the world's supply of cacao bean is now produced.

Production of candies and other confections first took place on a large scale in England in the early 19th century. The American candymaking industry grew rapidly during the second half of the 19th century.

By the turn of the 20th century, there were more than 1,000 American companies producing more than $60 million in candies each year. At that time, most candies were in the form of penny candy sweets. By the 1920s, when the first chocolate candy bars were introduced, the candymaking industry was producing $500 million each year, employing more than 75,000 people. The use of machines and automated equipment in the candymaking process has since reduced the number of people needed to produce candy. At the same time, the number of candymaking firms has dropped, with many smaller firms consolidating into large corporations.

The Job

Confectionery workers operate machines to mix and cook candy ingredients, to form candy mixtures into shapes, and to package them for sale. Many different machines are used to make the molded, filled, pulled, whipped, and coated candies that Americans consume. Even when the candymaking production line is completely automated, workers still are needed to monitor the various processing steps. However, some candy-making jobs, especially in smaller candy factories, are still done by hand.

Pantry workers assemble, weigh, and measure candy ingredients such as sugar, egg whites, and butter, following a fixed formula. To each batch of ingredients they attach a card denoting the formula used, so the next workers will know which candy is to be made from that batch.

Confectionery cookers cook candy mixtures according to a formula, using open-fire or steam-jacketed kettles or pressure cookers. They load ingredients into the machine and start the machine's agitator to mix them. They then set controls regulating the temperature and pressure at which the candy will be cooked and turn valves to admit steam or other heat. They may be responsible for checking the consistency of the batch and adjusting the sugar content if necessary. When the cooking is done they empty the batch onto slabs or cooling belts or into beaters.

Chocolate temperers melt chocolate using water-jacketed tempering kettles that alternately heat and cool the chocolate until it is the proper consistency. The workers who operate these machines regulate the temperature, mix and agitate the chocolate in the tank, and test the chocolate's viscosity, adding cocoa butter or lecithin as needed. This chocolate is used in molded candies or as a coating.

After the candy mixture is cooked, it is formed. Some candy is kneaded on slabs and cut into pieces. Rollers knead soft candy into rolls, which are cut into slices and shaped to form bonbon centers. *Rolling-machine operators* do a similar operation with machines, rolling slabs of candy to specified thicknesses before cutting. Candy spreaders pour and spread batches of cooked candy, such as fudge, caramel, and toffee, onto slabs or into trays before cutting and decorating. The cutting is sometimes done by a machine. *Cutting machine operators* select and install cutting disks according to the size and shape of candy pieces required. *Hand candy-cutters* cut pieces manually.

Other kinds of candy must be spun or pulled into rope-like strands before cutting. *Spinners* and *candy pullers* perform these tasks. A *center-machine operator* runs a machine that makes soft-candy centers for bonbons and chocolates. Other machines make different shapes. *Ball-machine operators* operate rolling machines that form candy balls and disks, and *lozenge makers* run machines that roll dough into sheets and then emboss and cut it into candy lozenges.

Many kinds of candy are made using molds. *Starch-makers* operate machines that make starch molds in which gum or jelly candy is formed. *Molding-machine operators* mold these candies using a mold-printing board. *Molding-machine operator helpers* feed the candy-filled starch molds onto conveyors or racks of machines that empty the molds, remove any remaining starch from the candies, and deposit candies in trays. *Hard-candy molders* pour liquid candy into chilled molds to form solid figures such as animals, people, and Christmas trees. *Chocolate Easter bunny makers* fill metal molds with chocolate, work in refrigerated rooms monitoring machines that spin the molds to coat them with the chocolate, and remove the Easter bunnies when the molds are sufficiently cooled. Another kind of hand molder is a *kiss setter*, who forms candy kisses using a spatula. *Deposit-machine operators* operate machines that deposit metered amounts of fluid candy into molds or directly onto conveyors. They must check the temperature and flow of the fluid and weigh formed candy samples to assure they meet specifications. *Fruit-bar makers* grind dried fruit and shape it into bars.

After candy centers are made, they must be coated, or enrobed. *Enrobing-machine feeders* arrange candy centers in a specified pattern on a conveyor, removing any malformed items. *Enrobing-machine operators* run machines that coat candy with melted chocolate or other coatings. They adjust the flow of coating mixture and allow coated candies to cool before further processing. In some plants, candy is dipped by hand workers, who scoop coating materials onto slabs and swirl center, fruits, or nuts through the coating and then remove them. Sometimes workers called *enrobing-machine corders* mark tops of machine-coated candies to simulate a hand-dipped appearance. They dip out a little semi-liquid chocolate out of a supply container and use it to draw a line or bead on the top of a newly enrobed piece of candy. Other workers do similar tasks. *Sanding-machine operators* sugar-coat gumdrops and orange slices. *Coating-machine operators* coat candy and nuts with syrup, coloring, or other materials to glaze or polish them.

Popcorn balls and flavored popcorn are also considered confections. *Corn poppers* operate gas ovens that pop corn. They measure corn, oil, and salt into the popper and remove the corn when it has popped. *Popcorn-candy makers* measure ingredients and cook flavored syrup, then coat popcorn with the syrup. *Cheese sprayers* spray cheese and coconut oil onto popcorn, salt it, and take it to the packing room. Some workers, including *decorators* and *garnishers*, use icing or nuts to decorate candy. Others make candy used to decorate other edibles. *Marzipan mixers* mix almond paste for marzipan cake decorations, which are formed by *marzipan molders*. *Casting-machine operators* form sugar decorations for cakes by forcing a sugar paste through a device for molding shapes, and depositing the decorations onto a paper sheet.

In some plants, *candy makers* are responsible for many of the steps in production, including formulating recipes and mixing, cooking, and forming candy. *Candy-maker helpers* help candy makers by tending machines, mixing ingredients, washing equipment, and performing other tasks. In large plants these jobs are often performed by different workers, under the direction of *candy supervisors*. Plants also employ *factory helpers*, who move trays from machine to machine and help confectionery workers in other ways.

After candy is formed, it is packaged, usually by machine, and delivered to distributors and eventually to retail stores.

Requirements

HIGH SCHOOL
A high school degree usually is required for jobs as confectionery industry workers. After they are hired, employees learn production skills on the job. High school courses in chemistry, biology, and shop are useful as background for some jobs, but skills are gained only through experience. Family and consumer science classes may offer the opportunity to learn about cooking, baking, and food products. For some advanced positions, such as candy maker, workers may need technical expertise in food chemistry or other fields, as well as a solid knowledge of the industry.

POSTSECONDARY TRAINING
For workers who want to advance to management positions, a bachelor's degree with an emphasis in food science technology and business courses is recommended.

OTHER REQUIREMENTS
Confectionery workers should have good manual dexterity. Like workers in many food industries, they may have to pass physical examinations to show that they are free from communicable diseases before they can begin work at a plant.

Exploring

If this type of work interests you, start exploring the field by making candy at home. Fudge, taffy, candied apples, and chocolate covered pretzels are among the sweets you can make in your own kitchen. Is there a candy manufacturing plant in your area? Call to see if tours are available. The Hershey chocolate plant in Hershey, Pennsylvania, for example, offers tours of their operation to the public. Get part-time or summer work at a candy store or the candy department of a large store where you can learn what products are popular, how the candy is stored and handled, and how to package it for customers. If there is a candy manufacturer in your area, you may be able to get part-time or summer work as a helper while you are still in high school.

Employers

A wide variety of settings are available to confectionery workers, from small candy stores that make their own confections to multinational corporations. Most of the approximately 48,000 candy manufacturing workers in the United States are employed at large plants. Employment is also available at small and mid-size confection manufacturers. Confectionery industry workers can find jobs in many parts of the United States.

Starting Out

Job seekers should apply directly to local plants for employment. Newspaper want ads and the state employment service are good sources of leads. In addition, the Bakery, Confectionery and Tobacco Workers International Union, to which many workers belong, may provide information about local openings. Some companies may place newspaper ads for workers. Many small retail stores, such as popcorn stores, also hire people to prepare and sell their candy and other confectionery products. Apply directly for these positions as well.

Advancement

Workers who are willing to learn about all aspects of confectionery making can advance to positions as candy makers or supervisors. Workers may enter other food processing occupations, such as raw sugar refining, where earnings may be considerably higher. The greater the range of specialized knowledge and skills a worker has, the greater the chance for advancement. The size of the plant and the rate of turnover among employees also affect promotion opportunities.

Earnings

Confectionery workers' wages vary widely depending on such factors as the workers' skills and the size and location of the plant. In general, workers on the West Coast earn more than those in other regions. According to the U.S. Department of Labor, weekly earnings for sugar and confectionery production workers average $594 in 2000. This wage translates into a yearly income of approximately $30,890. Since this amount is the average, there are both workers making more than this salary and workers making less. Entry-level, unskilled workers, such as helpers, may earn little more than the minimum wage, especially in smaller and nonunion factories. Those working full-time at the federal hourly minimum pay rate would have annual incomes of approximately $10,700. The U.S. Department of Labor also reports that mixing and blending machine operators, tenders, and setters earned a median hourly wage of $12.55 in 2000. A machine operator working full-time at this pay rate would have yearly earnings of approximately $26,105.

Confectionery workers typically receive such benefits as health insurance, time and a half pay for overtime, vacation days, and retirement plans.

Work Environment

Most confectionery workers in the United States work in large candy-making factories; many other workers are employed in plants with fewer than 20 workers. Most plants are modern, clean, and well lighted. Workers who tend machines must exercise caution, but working conditions generally are safe. The work is usually not physically demanding but can be tiring. Like many kinds of production work, some jobs in this field involve a great deal of repetition and routine, since each worker performs only a few tasks. Confectionery workers usually work 38 to 40 hours a week. They are often provided with uniforms to wear on the job.

Outlook

Candy sales in the United States are expected to hold about steady or perhaps increase slightly in coming years. Candy making, however, has become increasingly automated. It is often possible to produce candy products from the raw materials to the finished, packaged product without that product having ever been touched by human hands. As more and more confectionery producers adopt automated machinery and equipment, the need for production workers, especially unskilled workers without some college education, will decrease. In addition, the trend toward company consolidations will likely continue, meaning fewer employers of confectionery workers.

The U.S. Department of Labor projects an overall decline in the employment of food processing workers through 2010. Most new openings will arise as workers change jobs. Large wholesale confectionery companies will provide the most employment opportunities. Although candy is made throughout the United States, the candy industry is most active in Illinois, Pennsylvania, Ohio, New York, and California.

For More Information

The CMA, an affiliate of NCA, has information on cocoa farming, producing chocolate, links to processing and manufacturing companies, and other helpful information on its Web site.

CHOCOLATE MANUFACTURERS ASSOCIATION (CMA)
8320 Old Courthouse Road, Suite 300
Vienna, VA 22182
Tel: 703-790-5011
Web: http://www.chocolateandcocoa.org

The NCA provides the eCandy Marketplace, an online resource with information on such topics as confectionery products, candy manufacturers, research, and other industry news.

NATIONAL CONFECTIONERS ASSOCIATION (NCA)
8320 Old Courthouse Road, Suite 300
Vienna, VA 22182
Tel: 703-790-5750
Web: http://www.ecandy.com

This manufacturer's association provides information on scholarships available to undergraduate and graduate students and research news.

PENNSYLVANIA MANUFACTURING CONFECTIONERS ASSOCIATION
PO Box 176
Center Valley, PA 18034
Tel: 610-282-4640
Web: http://www.pmca.com

Cooks and Chefs

Quick Facts

School Subjects
Family and consumer science
Mathematics
Personal Skills
Artistic
Following instructions
Work Environment
Primarily indoors
Primarily one location
Minimum Education Level
Apprenticeship
Salary Range
$11,420 to $25,105 to $47,360+
Certification or Licensing
Required by certain states
Outlook
About as fast as the average

Overview

Cooks and *chefs* are employed in the preparation and cooking of food, usually in large quantities, in hotels, restaurants, cafeterias, and other establishments and institutions. There are more than 2.8 million cooks, chefs, and other food preparation workers employed in the United States.

History

The art of cookery is as ancient as the history of humankind. The early Greeks, Egyptians, and Romans valued cooks as highly respected members of society. France has given the world some of the finest cooks and chefs. Historical records reflect the avid interest the French people have in the art of cookery. Even today, cooks and chefs who are skilled in the art of French cuisine are highly valued and work in some of the world's most luxurious hotels and restaurants.

The hostelries of early America provided food and rest for weary travelers. Although these inns and taverns sometimes employed cooks specially hired from outside the proprietor's family, the food was often marginal in quality. It was not until hotels were built in the large cities that the occupation of cook developed into a profession.

The pleasure of dining out has become big business in the United States. The public has a range of choices—from the simplest, most inexpensive meal to the most expensive and elaborate. Whether a restaurant prides itself on "home cooking" or on exotic foreign cuisine, its cooks and chefs are largely responsible for the reputation it acquires.

The Job

Cooks and chefs are primarily responsible for the preparation and cooking of foods. Chefs usually supervise the work of cooks; however, the skills required and the job duties performed by each may vary depending upon the size and type of establishment.

Cooks and chefs begin by planning menus in advance. They estimate the amount of food that will be required for a specified period of time, order it from various suppliers, and check it for quantity and quality when it arrives. Following recipes or their own instincts, they measure and mix ingredients for soups, salads, gravies, sauces, casseroles, and desserts. They prepare meats, poultry, fish, vegetables, and other foods for baking, roasting, broiling, and steaming. They may use blenders, mixers, grinders, slicers, or tenderizers to prepare the food, and ovens, broilers, grills, roasters, or steam kettles to cook it. During the mixing and cooking, cooks and chefs rely on their judgment and experience to add seasonings; they constantly taste and smell food being cooked and must know when it is cooked properly. To fill orders, they carve meat, arrange food portions on serving plates, and add appropriate gravies, sauces, or garnishes.

Some larger establishments employ specialized cooks, such as banquet cooks, pastry cooks, and broiler cooks. The *garde-manger* designs and prepares buffets, and *pantry cooks* prepare cold dishes for lunch and dinner. Other specialists are raw shellfish preparers and carvers.

In smaller establishments without specialized cooks, kitchen helpers, or prep cooks, the general cooks may have to do some of the preliminary work themselves, such as washing, peeling, cutting, and shredding vegetables and fruits; cutting, trimming, and boning meat; cleaning and preparing poultry, fish, and shellfish; and baking bread, rolls, cakes, and pastries.

Commercial cookery is usually done in large quantities, and many cooks, including school cafeteria cooks and mess cooks, are trained in "quantity cookery" methods. Numerous establishments today are noted for their specialties in foods, and some cooks work exclusively in the preparation and cooking of exotic dishes, very elaborate meals, or some particular creation of their own for which they have become famous. Restaurants that feature national cuisines may employ international and regional cuisine specialty cooks.

In the larger commercial kitchens, chefs may be responsible for the work of a number of cooks, each preparing and cooking food in specialized areas. They may, for example, employ expert cooks who specialize in frying, baking, roasting, broiling, or sauce cookery. Cooks are often titled by the kinds of specialized cooking they do, such as fry, vegetable, or pastry. Chefs have the major responsibility for supervising the overall preparation and cooking of the food.

Other duties of chefs may include training cooks on the job, planning menus, pricing food for menus, and purchasing food. Chefs may be responsible for determining the weights of portions to be prepared and served. They may supervise the work of all members of the kitchen staff. The kitchen staff may assist by washing, cleaning, and preparing foods for cooking; cleaning utensils, dishes, and silverware; and assisting in many ways with the overall order and cleanliness of the kitchen. Most chefs spend part of their time creating new recipes that will win the praise of customers and build their reputations as experts.

Expert chefs who have a number of years of experience behind them may be employed as *executive chefs.* These chefs do little cooking or food preparation—their main responsibilities are management and supervision. Executive chefs interview, hire, and dismiss kitchen personnel, and they are sometimes responsible for the dining room waiters and other employees. These chefs consult with the restaurant manager regarding the profits and losses of the food service and ways to increase business and cut costs. A part of their time is spent inspecting equipment. Executive chefs are in charge of all food services for special functions such as banquets and parties, and they spend many hours in coordinating the work for these activities. They may supervise the special chefs and assist them in planning elaborate arrangements and creations in food preparation. Executive chefs may be assisted by workers called *sous chefs.*

Smaller restaurants may employ only one or two cooks and workers to assist them. Cooks and assistants work together to prepare all the food for cooking and to keep the kitchen clean. Because smaller restaurants and public eating places usually offer standard menus with little variation, the cook's job becomes standardized. Such establishments may employ specialty cooks, barbe-cue cooks, pizza bakers, food order expediters, kitchen food assemblers, or counter supply workers. In some restaurants food is cooked as it is ordered; cooks preparing food in this manner are known as *short-order cooks.*

Regardless of the duties performed, cooks and chefs are largely responsible for the reputation and monetary profit or loss of the eating establishment in which they are employed.

Requirements

The occupation of chef or cook has specific training requirements. Many cooks start out as kitchen helpers and acquire their skills on the job, but the trend today is to obtain training through high schools, vocational schools, or community colleges.

The amount of training required varies with the position. It takes only a short time to become an assistant or a fry cook, for example, but it requires years of training and experience to acquire the skills necessary to become an executive chef or cook in a fine restaurant.

HIGH SCHOOL

Although a high school diploma is not required for beginning posi-tions, it is an asset to job applicants. If you are interested in mov-ing beyond low-level positions such as kitchen helper or fry cook, your high school education should include classes in family and consumer science and health. These courses will teach you about nutrition, food preparation, and food storage. Math classes are also recommended; in this line of work you must be comfortable working with fractions, multiplying, and dividing. Since chefs and head cooks often have management responsibilities, you should also take business courses.

POSTSECONDARY TRAINING

Culinary students spend most of their time learning to prepare food through hands-on practice. At the same time, they learn how to use and care for kitchen equipment. Training programs often include courses in menu planning, determining portion size, con-trolling food costs, purchasing food supplies in quantity, selecting and storing food, and using leftovers. Students also learn hotel and restaurant sanitation and public health rules for handling food. Courses offered by private vocational schools, professional associations, and university programs often emphasize training in supervisory and management skills.

Professional associations and trade unions sometimes offer apprenticeship programs; one example is the three-year apprenticeship program sponsored by chapters of the American Culinary Federation (ACF) in cooperation with local employers. This program combines classroom work with on-the-job training under the supervision of a qualified chef and is an excellent way to begin your career. For more information, visit the education section of the ACF Web site http://www.acfchefs.org. Some large hotels and restaurants have their own training programs for new employees. The armed forces also offer good training and experience.

CERTIFICATION OR LICENSING

To protect the public's health, chefs, cooks, and bakers are required by law in most states to possess a health certificate and to be examined periodically. These examinations, usually given by the state board of health, make certain that the individual is free from communicable diseases and skin infections. ACF offers certification at a variety of levels, such as executive chef and sous chef. In addition to educational and experience requirements, candidates must also pass written tests for each certification. Certification from ACF is recommended as a way to enhance your professional standing and advance your career.

OTHER REQUIREMENTS

The successful chef or cook has a keen interest in food preparation and cooking and has a desire to experiment with new recipes and new food combinations. You should be able to work as part of a team and work under pressure during rush hours, in close quarters, and with a certain amount of noise and confusion.

Immaculate personal cleanliness and good health are necessities in this trade. You should possess physical stamina and be without serious physical impairments because of the mobility and activity the work requires. You will spend many working hours standing, walking, and moving about.

Chefs and cooks must possess a keen sense of taste and smell. Hand and finger agility, hand-eye coordination, and a good memory are helpful. An artistic flair and creative talents in working with food are definitely strengths in this trade.

The principal union for cooks and chefs is the Hotel Employees and Restaurant Employees International Union (affiliated with the AFL-CIO).

Exploring

You may explore your interest in cooking right at home. Prepare meals for your family, offer to make a special dessert for a friend's birthday, create your own recipes. Any hands-on experience will build your skills and help you determine what type of cooking you enjoy the most.

Volunteer opportunities may be available at local kitchens that serve to the homeless or others in need. You can also get a paying part-time or summer job at a fast food or other restaurant. Large and institutional kitchens, for example those in nursing homes, may offer positions such as sandwich or salad maker, soda-fountain attendant, or kitchen helper.

Employers

Cooks and chefs are needed by restaurants of all types and sizes; schools, hospitals, and other institutions; hotels, cruise lines, airlines, and other industries; and catering and bakery businesses. Approximately 60 percent work at restaurants, other retail eateries, and drinking establishments. Roughly 20 percent are employed by institutions/cafeterias, such as schools, hospitals, and nursing homes. The remainder work at such places as grocery stores, hotels, and catering businesses.

Starting Out

Apprenticeship programs are one method of entering the trade. These programs usually offer the beginner sound basic training and a regular salary. Upon completion of the apprenticeship, cooks may be hired full-time in their place of training or assisted in finding employment with another establishment. Cooks are hired as chefs only after they have acquired a number of years of experience.

Cooks who have been formally trained through public or private trade or vocational schools or in culinary institutes may be able to take advantage of school placement services.

In many cases, a cook begins as a kitchen helper or cook's helper and, through experience gained in on-the-job training, is able to move into the job of cook. To do this, people sometimes start out in small restaurants, perhaps as short-order cooks, grill cooks, or sandwich or salad makers, and transfer to larger establishments as they gain experience.

School cafeteria workers who want to become cooks may have an opportunity to receive food-services training. Many school districts, with the cooperation of school food-services divisions of the state departments of education, provide on-the-job training and sometimes summer workshops for interested cafeteria employees. Some community colleges, state departments of education, and school associations offer similar programs. Cafeteria workers who have completed these training programs are often selected to fill positions as cooks.

Job opportunities may be located through employment bureaus, trade associations, unions, contacts with friends, newspaper want ads, or local offices of the state employment service. Another method is to apply directly to restaurants or hotels. Small restaurants, school cafeterias, and other eating places with simple food preparation will provide the greatest number of starting jobs for cooks. Job applicants who have had courses in commercial food preparation will have an advantage in large restaurants and hotels, where hiring standards are often high.

Advancement

Advancement depends on the skill, training, experience, originality, and ambition of the individual. It also depends somewhat on the general business climate and employment trends.

Cooks with experience can advance by moving to other places of employment for higher wages or to establishments looking for someone with a specialized skill in preparing a particular kind of food. Cooks who have a number of years of successful job experience may find chef positions open to them; however, in some cases it may take 10 or 15 years to obtain such a position, depending on personal qualifications and other employment factors.

Expert cooks who have obtained supervisory responsibilities as head cooks or chefs may advance to positions as executive chefs or to other types of managerial work. Some go into business for themselves as caterers or restaurant owners; others may become instructors in vocational programs in high schools, colleges, or other academic institutions.

Earnings

The salaries earned by chefs and cooks depend on many factors, such as the size, type, and location of the establishment, and the skill, experience, training, and specialization of the worker. Salaries are usually fairly standard among establishments of the same type. For example, restaurants and diners serving inexpensive meals and a sandwich-type menu generally pay cooks less than establishments with medium-priced or expensive menus. The highest wages are earned at restaurants known for their elegance.

According to the U.S. Department of Labor, in 2000, the median hourly wage for head cooks and chefs was $12.07. Based on a 40-hour workweek and full year employment, a person paid this hourly amount would have a yearly income of approximately $25,105. The highest paid 10 percent of head cooks and chefs earned more than $22.77 per hour, or more than $47,360 per year. Restaurant cooks had a median hourly wage of $8.72, or approximate annual earnings of $18,135. Cooks working at institutions or cafeterias had a median of $8.22 per hour (approximately $17,098 per year). Short-order cooks earned a median hourly wage of $7.55 (approximately $15,700 annually). Cooks at fast food restaurants were at the bottom of the pay scale, earning a median of $6.53 per hour (approximately $13,580 per year); the lowest paid 10 percent of these cooks earned less than $5.49 per hour (approximately $11,420 annually).

Chefs and cooks usually receive their meals free during working hours and are furnished with any necessary job uniforms. Full-time workers usually receive health insurance and vacation and sick days.

Work Environment

Working conditions vary with the place of employment. Many kitchens are modern, well lighted, well equipped, and air-conditioned, but some older, smaller eating places may be only marginally equipped. The work of cooks can be strenuous, with long hours of standing, lifting heavy pots, and working near hot ovens and ranges. Possible hazards include falls, cuts, and burns, although serious injury is uncommon. Even in the most modern kitchens, cooks, chefs, and bakers usually work amid considerable noise from the operation of equipment and machinery.

Chefs and cooks may work a 40- or 48-hour week, depending on the type of food service offered and certain union agreements. Some food establishments are open 24 hours a day, while others may be open from the very early morning until late in the evening. Establishments open long hours may have two or three work shifts, with some chefs and cooks working day schedules while others work evenings.

All food-service workers may have to work overtime hours, depending on the amount of business and rush-hour trade. These employees work many weekends and holidays, although they may have a day off every week or rotate with other employees to have alternate weekends free. Many cooks are required to work early morning or late evening shifts. For example, doughnuts, breads, and muffins for breakfast service must be baked by 6 or 7 AM, which requires bakers to begin work at 2 or 3 AM. Some people will find it very difficult to adjust to working such late and irregular hours.

Outlook

Overall the employment of chefs and cooks is expected to increase as fast as the average for all occupations through 2010, according to the U.S. Department of Labor. While some areas (such as cooks in fast food) may not see much growth in number of new jobs, turnover rates are high and the need to find replacement cooks and chefs will mean many job opportunities in all areas. The need for cooks and chefs will also grow as the population increases and lifestyles change. As people earn higher incomes and have more leisure time, they dine out more often and take more vacations. In addition, working parents and their families dine out frequently as a convenience.

For More Information

For information on careers in baking and cooking, education, and certification, contact the following organizations:

AMERICAN CULINARY FEDERATION, INC.
10 San Bartola Drive
St. Augustine, FL 32086
Tel: 800-624-9458
Web: http://www.acfchefs.org

AMERICAN INSTITUTE OF BAKING
PO Box 3999
1213 Bakers Way
Manhattan, KS 66505-3999
Tel: 800-633-5137
Web: http://www.aibonline.org

CULINARY INSTITUTE OF AMERICA
1946 Campus Drive
Hyde Park, NY 12538-1499
Tel: 845-452-9600
Web: http://www.ciachef.edu

EDUCATIONAL INSTITUTE OF THE AMERICAN HOTEL AND LODGING ASSOCIATION
800 North Magnolia Avenue, Suite 1800
Orlando, FL 32803
Tel: 800-752-4567
Web: http://www.ei-ahla.org

NATIONAL RESTAURANT ASSOCIATION EDUCATIONAL FOUNDATION
175 West Jackson Boulevard, Suite 1500
Chicago, IL 60604-2702
Tel: 800-765-2122
Web: http://www.nraef.org

For information on culinary schools in Canada, industry news, and a job bank, visit this organization's Web site.
CANADIAN FEDERATION OF CHEFS AND COOKS
Box 91459
West Vancouver, BC V7V 3P1 Canada
Tel: 604-922-9498
Web: http://www.cfcc.ca

Dairy Products Workers

Quick Facts

School Subjects
  Agriculture
  Biology
  Chemistry
Personal Skills
  Following instructions
  Technical/scientific
Work Environment
  Primarily indoors
  Primarily one location
Minimum Education Level
  High school diploma
Salary Range
  $12,400 to $28,184 to $43,020+
Certification or Licensing
  Required by all states
Outlook
  Decline

Overview

Dairy products workers set up, operate, and tend continuous-flow or vat-type equipment to process milk, cream, butter, cheese, ice cream, and other dairy products following specified methods and formulas.

History

Since herd animals were first domesticated, humankind has kept cattle for meat and milk. From its ancient beginnings in Asia, the practice of keeping cattle spread across much of the world. Often farmers kept a few cows to supply their family's dairy needs. Because fresh milk spoils easily, milk that was not consumed as a beverage had to be made into a product like cheese. Before the invention of refrigeration, cheese was the only dairy product that could be easily transported across long distances. Over the centuries, many distinctive types of hard cheeses have become associated with various regions of the world, such as Cheddar from England, Edam and Gouda from Holland, Gruyere from Switzerland, and Parmesan and Provolone from Italy.

A real dairy products industry has evolved only in the last century or so, with the development of refrigeration and various kinds of specialized processing machinery, the scientific study of cattle breeding, and improved road and rail transportation systems for distributing manufactured products. The rise in urban popula-

tions also gave an extra impetus to the growth of the industry, as more and more people moved away from farm sources of dairy products and into cities.

Another important advancement was the introduction of pasteurization, named for the noted French chemist Louis Pasteur (1822-95). Many harmful bacteria can live in fresh milk. In the 1860s, Pasteur developed the process of pasteurization, which involves heating a foodstuff to a certain temperature for a specified period of time to kill the bacteria, then cooling the food again.

The Job

Dairy products workers handle a wide variety of machines that process milk, manufacture dairy products, and prepare the products for shipping. Workers are usually classified by the type of machine they operate. Workers at some plants handle more than one type of machine.

Whole milk is delivered to a dairy processing plant from farms in large containers or in special tank trucks. The milk is stored in large vats until *dairy processing equipment operators* are ready to use it. First, the operator connects the vats to processing equipment with pipes, assembling whatever valves, bowls, plates, disks, impeller shafts, and other parts are needed to prepare the equipment for operation. Then the operator turns valves to pump a sterilizing solution and rinse water throughout the pipes and equipment. While keeping an eye on temperature and pressure gauges, the operator opens other valves to pump the whole milk into a centrifuge where it is spun at high speed to separate the cream from the skim milk. The milk is also pumped through a homogenizer to produce a specified emulsion (consistency that results from the distribution of fat through the milk) and, last, through a filter to remove any sediment. All this is done through continuous-flow machines.

The next step for the equipment operator is pasteurization, or the killing of bacteria that exist in the milk. The milk is heated by pumping steam or hot water through pipes in the pasteurization equipment. When it has been at the specified temperature for the correct length of time, a refrigerant is pumped through refrigerator coils in the equipment, which quickly brings the milk temperature down. Once the milk has been pasteurized, it is either bottled in glass, paper, or plastic containers, or it is pumped to other storage tanks for further processing. The dairy processing equipment operator may also add to the milk specified amounts of liquid or powdered ingredients, such as vitamins, lactic culture, stabilizer, or neutralizer, to make products such as buttermilk, yogurt, chocolate milk, or ice cream. The batch of milk is tested for acidity at various stages of this process, and each time the operator records the time, temperature, pressure, and volume readings for the milk. The operator may clean the equipment before processing the next batch of whole milk.

Processed milk includes a lot of nonfat dry milk, which is far easier to ship and store than fresh milk. Dry milk is produced in a gas-fired drier tended by a *drier operator.* The drier operator first turns on the equipment's drier mechanism, vacuum pump, and circulating fan and adjusts the flow controls. Once the proper drier temperature is reached, a pump sprays liquid milk into the heated vacuum chamber where milk droplets dry to powder and fall to the bottom of the chamber. The drier operator tests the dried powder for the proper moisture content and the chamber walls for burnt scale, which indicates excessive temperatures and appears as undesirable sediment when the milk is reconstituted. *Milk-powder grinders* operate equipment that mills and sifts the milk powder, ensuring a uniform texture.

For centuries, butter was made by hand in butter churns in which cream was agitated with a plunger until pieces of butter congealed and separated from the milk. Modern butter-making machines perform the same basic operation on a much larger scale. After sterilizing the machine, the *butter maker* starts a pump that admits a measured amount of pasteurized cream into the churn. The butter maker activates the churn and, as the cream is agitated by paddles, monitors the gradual separation of the butter from the milk. Once the process is complete, the milk is pumped out and stored, and the butter is sprayed with chlorinated water to remove excess remaining milk. With testing apparatus, the butter maker determines the butter's moisture and salt content and adjusts the consistency by adding or removing water. Finally, the butter maker examines the color and smells and tastes the butter to grade it according to predetermined standards.

In addition to the churn method, butter can also be produced by a chilling method. In this process, the butter maker pasteurizes and separates cream to obtain butter oil. The butter oil is tested in a standardizing vat for its levels of butter fat, moisture, salt content, and acidity. The butter maker adds appropriate amounts of water, alkali, and coloring to the butter oil and starts an agitator to mix the ingredients. The resulting mix is chilled in a vat at a specified temperature until it congeals into butter.

Cheesemakers cook milk and other ingredients according to formulas to make cheese. The cheesemaker first fills a cooking vat with milk of a prescribed butterfat content, heats the milk to a specified temperature, and dumps in measured amounts of dye and starter culture. The mixture is agitated and tested for acidity, which affects the rate at which enzymes coagulate milk proteins and produce cheese. When a certain level of acidity has been reached, the cheesemaker adds a measured amount of rennet, a substance containing milk-curdling enzymes. The milk is left alone to coagulate into curd, the thick, protein-rich part of milk used to make cheese. The cheesemaker later releases the whey, the watery portion of the milk, by pulling curd knives through the curd or using a hand scoop. Then the curd is agitated in the vat and cooked for a period of time, with the cheesemaker squeezing and stretching samples of curd by hand and adjusting the cooking time to achieve the desired firmness or texture. Once this is done, the cheesemaker or a *cheesemaker helper* drains the whey from the curd, adds ingredients such as seasonings, and then molds, packs, cuts, piles, mills, and presses the curd into specified shapes. To make certain types of cheese, the curd may be immersed in brine, rolled in dry salt, pierced or smeared with a culture solution to develop mold growth, or placed on shelves to be cured. Later, the cheesemaker samples the cheese for its taste, smell, look, and feel. Sampling and grading is also done by *cheese graders*, experts in cheeses who are required to have a state or federal license.

The distinctive qualities of various kinds of cheeses depend on a number of factors, including the kind and condition of the milk, the cheesemaking process, and the method and duration of curing. For example, cottage cheese is made by the method described above. However, the *cottage cheese maker* starts the temperature low and slowly increases it. When the curd reaches the proper consistency, the cottage cheese maker stops the cooking process and drains off the whey. This method accounts for cottage cheese's loose consistency. Cottage cheese and other soft cheeses are not cured like hard cheeses and are meant for immediate consumption.

Process cheese products are made by blending and cooking different cheeses, cheese curd, or other ingredients such as cream, vegetable shortening, sodium citrate, and disodium phosphate. The *process cheese cooker* dumps the various ingredients into a vat and cooks them at a prescribed temperature. When the mixture reaches a certain consistency, the cooker pulls a lever to drain the cheese into a hopper or bucket. The process cheese may be pumped through a machine that makes its texture finer. Unheated cheese or curd may be mixed with other ingredients to make cold pack cheese or cream cheese. Other cheese workers include *casting-machine operators,* who tend the machines that form, cool, and cut the process cheese into slices of a specified size and weight, and *grated-cheese makers,* who handle the grinding, drying, and cooling equipment that makes grated cheese.

Ice cream is usually made from milk fat, nonfat milk solids, sweeteners, stabilizer (usually gelatin), and flavorings such as syrup, nuts, and fruit. Ice cream can be made in individual batches by *batch freezers* or in continuous-mix equipment by *freezer operators.* In the second method, the freezer operator measures the dry and liquid ingredients, such as the milk, coloring, flavoring, or fruit puree, and dumps them into the flavor vat. The mix is blended, pumped into freezer barrels, and injected with air. In the freezer barrel, the mix is agitated and scraped from the freezer walls while it slowly hardens. The operator then releases the ice cream through a valve outlet that may inject flavored syrup for rippled ice cream. The ice cream is transferred to a filling machine that pumps it into cartons, cones, cups, or molds for pies, rolls, and tarts. Other workers may process the ice cream into its various types, such as cones, varicolored packs, and special shapes. These workers include *decorators, novelty makers, flavor room workers,* and *sandwich-machine operators.*

Newly hired inexperienced workers in a dairy processing plant may start out as *dairy helpers,* or *cheese making laborers.* Beginning workers may do any of a wide variety of support tasks, such as scrubbing and sterilizing bottles and equipment, attaching pipes and fittings to machines, packing cartons, weighing containers, and moving stock. If they prove to be reliable, workers may be given more responsibility and assigned tasks such as filling tanks with milk or ingredients, examining canned milk for dirt or odor, monitoring machinery, cutting and wrapping butter and cheese, or filling cartons or bags with powdered milk. In time, workers may be trained to operate and repair any of the specialized processing machines found in the factory.

The raw milk at a dairy processing plant is supplied by *dairy farmers*, who raise and tend milk-producing livestock, usually cows. Dairy farmers often own their own farms, breed their own cows, and use special equipment to milk the cows, often twice a day. Many also perform other farm-related tasks, including growing crops. Assisting the dairy farmer is the *dairy herd supervisor*, who takes milk samples from cows and tests the milk samples for information such as the amount of fat, protein, and other solids present in the milk. The dairy herd supervisor helps the farmer make certain that each cow in the herd is healthy and that the milk it produces will be fit for human consumption. Dairy herd supervisors do not generally work for one dairy farmer, but rather oversee the milk production at a number of farms.

Requirements

HIGH SCHOOL
Most dairy products workers learn their skills from company training sessions and on-the-job experience. Employers prefer to hire workers with at least a high school education. Courses that can provide helpful background for work in this field include mathematics, biology, and chemistry. Machine shop classes also can be useful to prepare for handling and repairing heavy machinery.

POSTSECONDARY TRAINING
Students interested in becoming cheesemakers may find it necessary to obtain a college degree in a food technology or food science program. Dairy herd supervisors, in addition to a two-year or four-year food technology or food science degree, should try to gain experience working on a dairy farm. Those who seek management positions may need a bachelor's degree in food manufacturing with an emphasis on accounting, management, and business.

CERTIFICATION OR LICENSING
To ensure that consumers are receiving safe, healthful dairy foods, many dairy products workers must be licensed by a state board of

health or other local government unit. Licensing is intended to guarantee workers' knowledge of health laws, their skills in handling equipment, and their ability to grade the quality of various goods according to established standards. Some workers, such as cheese graders, may need to be licensed by the federal government as well.

OTHER REQUIREMENTS

Many dairy products workers must pass physical examinations and receive certificates stating they are free from contagious diseases. An interest in food products and manual dexterity in operating equipment are important characteristics for this work.

Exploring

People who think they may be interested in working in the dairy products manufacturing industry may be able to find summer jobs as helpers in dairy processing plants. Assisting or at least observing equipment operators, cheesemakers, butter makers, and others as they work is a good way to learn about this field. High school students may also find part-time or summer employment at dairy farms.

Starting Out

A good place to find information about job openings is at the personnel offices of local dairy processing plants. Other sources of information include newspaper classified ads and the offices of the state employment service. Those with associate's or bachelor's degrees in food technology, food science, or a related program can apply directly to dairy processing plants; many schools offering such programs provide job placement assistance. Dairy farmers often begin their careers by working on their own family farms.

Advancement

After gaining some experience, dairy products workers may advance to become shift supervisors or production supervisors. Advancement is usually limited to those with at least an associate's or bachelor's degree in a food technology, food science, or related course of study. Formal training in related fields is necessary in order to move up to such positions as laboratory technician, plant engineer, or plant manager.

Workers who wish to change industries may find that many of their skills can be transferred to other types of food processing. With further training and education, they may become dairy plant inspectors or technicians employed by local or state health departments.

Earnings

According to *Dairy USA Wage Survey 2000* compiled by Gregorio Billikopf Encina at the University of California, milkers earned average wages of $9.26 an hour, and wages ranged from $6 to $13.12. Herd managers averaged $10.36 an hour and wages ranged from $5.36 to $13.34. Cow feeders earned wages ranging from $5.75 to $12.50 an hour, with an average of $9.20 an hour. Dairy farm workers are sometimes offered incentives and bonuses for improved milk quality and production and overall performance. Dairy workers usually receive benefits, including paid vacation and sick leave and insurance packages. Some employers provide housing or a housing allowance.

The U.S. Department of Labor reports that full-time, salaried farm managers had median weekly earnings of $542 ($28,184 annually) in 2000. Earnings ranged from less than $187 to more than $756. Incomes of dairy farmers vary greatly from year to year because prices of farm products fluctuate according to the quantity and quality of milk products and the demand for them. The 1996 Farm Act phases out government price supports for dairy farmers, and may result in lower incomes for dairy producers.

In the food processing industry, supervisors and managers of production workers earned a mean salary of $43,020 a year in 2000, according to the Bureau of Labor Statistics. Food batchmakers earned about $22,280 and food cooking machine operators and tenders earned $21,830. Full-time workers usually receive a full benefits package.

Work Environment

Because of the strict health codes and sanitary standards to which they must adhere, dairy plants are generally clean, well-ventilated workplaces, equipped with modern, well-maintained machines. When workplace safety rules are followed, dairy processing plants are not hazardous places to work.

Workers in this industry generally report for work as early as 6 AM, with shifts ending around three in the afternoon. Dairy farmers and others may start work as early as four or five in the morning. People involved in the agriculture industry often work very long hours, often more than 12 hours per day. Many dairy products workers stand during most of their workday. In some positions the work is very repetitive. Although the milk itself is generally transported from tank to tank via pipelines, some workers have to lift and carry other heavy items, such as cartons of flavoring, emulsifier, chemical additives, and finished products like cheese. To clean vats and other equipment, some workers have to get inside storage tanks and spray the walls with hot water, chemicals, or live steam.

Dairy workers may also be exposed to health risks associated with working with animals and animal products, such as bacteria and other organisms.

Outlook

The 1996 Federal Agriculture Improvement and Reform Act (also known as the 1996 Farm Act) was enacted to phase out price supports for agricultural produce. The Act also called for replacing the federal price support system for milk with new loan programs beginning in the year 2000, allowing the milk prices received by dairy farmers to be determined by market forces. Only the larger, more financially sound farms will be able to compete in international and domestic markets. This is likely to continue to force owners of smaller farms to consolidate with larger operations or leave agricultural production altogether. According to the American Farm Bureau, the nation has lost more than 40,000 licensed dairies since 1992. Farmer-owned and -operated cooperatives are developing new ways to market milk, dairy products, and other agricultural produce and these efforts hold some promise for dairy and other farms.

The U.S. Department of Labor expects a 7.8 percent decline in overall employment in agricultural production through 2010. The decline will be fastest (at 14 percent) among self-employed and unpaid family workers, most of whom are farmers. Employment of wage and salary workers will decline 2.5 percent. Overall wage and salary employment in food processing is expected to decline by about 3 percent over the 2000-10 period.

For More Information

The following organization has a journal, a student affiliate, and information about the dairy industry.
AMERICAN DAIRY SCIENCE ASSOCIATION
1111 North Dunlap Avenue
Savoy, IL 61874
Tel: 217-356-3182
Web: http://www.adsa.uiuc.edu

For information about the dairy industry and the American Dairy Association, the National Dairy Council, and the U.S. Dairy Export Council, contact:
DAIRY MANAGEMENT, INC.
10255 West Higgins Road, Suite 900
Rosemont, IL 60018-5616
Web: http://www.dairyinfo.com

The following is a federation of the Milk Industry Foundation, National Cheese Institute, and the International Ice Cream Association.
INTERNATIONAL DAIRY FOODS ASSOCIATION
1250 H Street, NW, Suite 900
Washington, DC 20005
Tel: 202-737-4332
Web: http://www.idfa.org

The following organization is concerned with milk quality and standards, animal health and food safety issues, dairy product labeling and standards, and legislation affecting the dairy industry.
NATIONAL MILK PRODUCERS FEDERATION
2101 Wilson Boulevard, Suite 400
Arlington, VA 22201
Tel: 703-243-6111
Web: http://www.nmpf.org

Enologists

Quick Facts

School Subjects
  Biology
  Chemistry
  Computer science
Personal Skills
  Following instructions
  Technical/scientific
Work Environment
  Indoors and outdoors
  Primarily one location
Minimum Education Level
  High school diploma
  Apprenticeship
Salary Range
  $25,000 to $36,500
  to $200,000+
Certification or Licensing
  None available
Outlook
  Faster than the average

Overview

Enologists, or *wine makers,* direct and manage most activities of a winery, including planting grapes and producing, storing, and shipping wine. They select the type of grapes grown and supervise workers in the production process from harvesting to fermenting, aging, and bottling. Enologists work with different varieties of grapes in a type or species to develop the strongest and most flavorful wines.

History

Wine making has been practiced for more than 5,000 years. Ancient Egyptians had hieroglyphics representing wine making, and it was an important commodity in Palestine during the time of Jesus. The Chinese made wine more than 4,000 years ago as did the Greeks and Romans.

Throughout history, wine has been used as a drink to accompany meals or as part of religious practices. In fact, the use of wine spread throughout Europe because of its use in religious services. Wine also was used as a medicine or curative.

Grapes have been cultivated in the United States since the late 1700s. Enology or viticulture, the cultivation of grapes, is a major industry now, primarily in California, the Pacific Northwest and the Northeast. More than 80 percent of the U.S. domestic wine is cultivated in California. Enologists have played an instrumental role in the growth of the wine industry, experimenting with different types of grapes and growing conditions and improving the quality of wines produced.

The Job

Enologists are involved in all aspects of wine production and therefore must have a thorough knowledge of the winemaking business. They must be able to analyze the quality of grapes, decide which vines are best to grow, determine when grapes are ripe enough to be picked, and coordinate the process of winemaking. Production decisions include which yeast or bacteria to use, at what temperature fermentation should occur, and how the wine is to be aged.

Selection of the proper grapes is a vital part of an enologist's planning responsibilities. This selection process includes analyzing the varieties of grapes to determine which are best suited to grow in a specific area, given existing soil and climate conditions. For example, an enologist in California must ensure that grapes chosen to grow in that climate can withstand the heat of the summers, while an enologist in New York must ensure that grapes chosen can withstand the cooler temperatures there. Other factors that determine which type of grapes to grow include the desired flavor and aroma of wines and the species' ability to withstand disease.

Grapes that produce red wine are processed in a different way than grapes that produce white wine. Production methods also vary according to the size of the winery and the type of containers and stainless steel tanks used in the crushing and fermentation processes. Enologists have the final word in all of the production decisions. They consult with other winery staff about issues involving the testing and crushing of grapes, the cooling, filtering, and bottling of the wine, and the type of storage casks in which to place the wine. The enologist also researches and implements modifications in growing and production techniques to ensure the best quality product at the lowest cost. This involves keeping up with technological improvements in production methods and the ability to read and analyze a profit-and-loss statement and other parts of a balance sheet.

Enologists oversee personnel matters. They may hire and train employees such as vineyard and production workers, coordinate work schedules, and develop a salary structure. Good communication skills are needed to present written and oral reports.

Although bookkeeping, reporting to government agencies, and other administrative tasks often are delegated to an assistant, enologists must have an understanding of industry regulations, accounting, and mathematics. Production costs and other expenses must be carefully recorded. Because of the increased use of computers for recording composition and grape details, blending and production alternatives, and analyzing information, enologists should have some training in computer science.

An enologist sometimes is involved with decisions regarding the marketing of the finished product. Production, transportation, and distribution costs, the potential markets on the national and international level, and other factors must be calculated to determine the price of the finished wine and where the wine will be sold.

Requirements

HIGH SCHOOL
In high school, you should take courses in mathematics, biology, chemistry, and physics. You should also take English and other courses that enhance communication skills. Foreign languages, particularly French and German, may enhance opportunities for study or research abroad.

POSTSECONDARY TRAINING
Although some wineries offer on-the-job training in the form of apprenticeships for high school graduates, the majority of entry-level positions go to college graduates. A bachelor's degree in enology or viticulture is preferred, but a degree in food or fermentation science or a related subject such as microbiology or biochemistry is acceptable. Specific courses related to winery management should include wine analysis and wine microbiology. Business, economics, marketing, and computer science should also be part of the degree program. There are enology programs at University of California at Davis, California State University at Fresno, and Cornell University. As competition in the field increases, many enologists are choosing to pursue a master's degree and to gain experience in related scientific research.

Although no licenses or certificates are necessary to work in the field, many enologists choose to continue professional enrichment through continuing education classes and affiliation with organizations such as the American Society for Enology and Viticulture.

OTHER REQUIREMENTS

Enologists need excellent verbal and written communication skills, and you must be able to handle multiple tasks and priorities. You must take direction from supervisors and work well on a team. Basic computer knowledge is important, as is familiarity with the Bureau of Alcohol, Tobacco and Firearms and state regulations concerning winemaking, handling, and transport.

Enologists must be familiar with safety equipment and procedures. You need the physical strength to climb stairs, work on high platforms, lift and carry 40 pounds, bend, squat, and stretch. Most wineries require you to be at least 21 years of age.

Exploring

Part-time or summer employment at a winery is an excellent method of gaining an insight into the skills and temperament needed for this profession. A high school student also can explore opportunities in the field through discussions with professionals already working as enologists. Because many technical colleges offer evening courses, it may be possible for a high school student to audit or take a course for future college credit.

Employers

Enologists are employed in a variety of settings, from small wineries to large manufacturing plants and multinational corporations. Some enologists may do research or quality assurance work. Since many vineyards and wineries are located in California, jobs are more abundant in that area.

Starting Out

The usual method of entry is to be hired by a winery after completing an undergraduate or graduate degree in enology, fermentation, or food science. Summer or part-time work sometimes may lead to a permanent job, and an apprenticeship program at the winery provides the necessary training.

Advancement

Advancement depends on performance, experience, and education. Enologists at small wineries may become managers at larger facilities. Those at larger facilities may move on to direct a number of wineries as part of a nationwide organization. A small number of enologists may start their own wineries. Because of the relatively small number of wineries in the country and the fact that enologists have high-level management positions from the start, advancement opportunities are somewhat limited.

Earnings

A survey of the wine industry by *Practical Winery & Vineyard* magazine (Jan/Feb 1998) reports that salaries ranged from a low of $14,000 for unskilled workers in the cellar or vineyard to highs of more than $200,000 for top winemakers and other executives at some larger wineries. Assistant winemaker is a typical position for an enology graduate with a few years experience. Median salaries in this position ranged from $36,500 at small wineries to $48,000 at large wineries. Median earnings for vineyard managers ranged from $31,000 to $56,000, depending on winery or vineyard size. Recent graduates of enology programs reported starting salaries between $30,000 and $40,000.

According to a 2001 Winebusiness.com salary survey, average salaries for presidents of wineries ranged from $47,600 to $245,000, depending on the size of the winery. Salaries for winery presidents of all size wineries ranged from $6,000 to $285,000. General managers' salaries ranged from $40,000 to $200,000 with a median salary of $50,000 for wineries producing 50,000 or fewer cases per year.

Work Environment

Enologists work mostly indoors, with some outdoor activities in a vineyard. Enologists enjoy variety in their jobs as they constantly alternate between analyzing the grapes in the field, assessing the development of wines, studying current production techniques, planning marketing strategies for the upcoming harvest, and other responsibilities. Physical labor such as lifting a 40-pound wine case or pruning a vineyard may be required.

During most of the year an enologist works 40 hours a week, but during the late summer and early fall when the grape harvest occurs, an enologist should expect to work long hours six or seven days a week for a four- to six-week period.

As a manager, an enologist should be able to communicate and work well with people. The ability to interpret data is vital as much of the enologist's planning responsibilities involve working with crop and market forecasts. Attention to detail is critical. An enologist should be able to spend long hours analyzing information and make and implement decisions concerning this information.

Outlook

Job growth is tied to the size and quality of grape harvests, the success of wine production, and the foreign and domestic demand for American wines. Technological advances in wine production may create more job opportunities. Total U.S. wine exports for July 2001 increased 32.18 percent in volume over July 2000, with especially rapid growth in sales to the United Kingdom and Belgium, according to Winebusiness.Com. Imports also increased 23.64 percent in volume, with the largest increases in imports from Italy, Australia, Chile, Argentina, and Hungary.

In 2001, California experienced its second-largest harvest of wine grapes, which may lead to surpluses and lower prices. However, it is impossible to predict weather and soil conditions from season to season and there is little security, especially for smaller wine producers. There is stiff competition in the wine business and there have been a number of consolidations and mergers in the past few years. Still, new brands continue to be introduced with strong marketing campaigns, particularly in the lower and mid-priced categories.

Job opportunities will be best in California, where most of the U.S. wineries are located. Most California wine is cultivated in the San Joaquin, Napa, and Sonoma valleys, the central coast, and the Sierra foothills.

For More Information

For information on various aspects of winemaking, contact:
AMERICAN SOCIETY FOR ENOLOGY AND VITICULTURE
PO Box 1855
Davis, CA 95617
Tel: 530-753-3142
Web: http://www.asev.org

For information on education and chapter events, including competitions and wine tastings, contact:
AMERICAN WINE SOCIETY
3006 Latta Road
Rochester, NY 14612
Tel: 716-225-7613
Web: http://www.vicon.net/~aws

Family and
Consumer Scientists

Overview

Family and consumer scientists, also called *home economists,* improve and help others to improve products, services, and practices that affect the comfort and well-being of the home and family. Family and consumer science covers a range of subjects from nutrition, food preparation, and meal planning to household economics and the psychology of family relations. All the aspects of household and home management are part of this broad field.

History

The field of family and consumer science—or domestic science, as it was called—developed in the late 1800s, as more women began to pursue education. By 1890, the subject was taught in most public schools, colleges, and universities. The most important step in the establishment of this field was the Morrill Act of 1862, which made possible the land-grant colleges, where family and consumer science achieved much of its growth and stature through research, teaching, and extension services. Many of these colleges did and still do refer to these programs as home economics.

Today the field of family and consumer science has expanded into every segment of family life. Families look to the family and consumer scientist for expert advice through consumer magazines, radio and television programs, home bureaus, university extension centers, and adult education courses. Experts in this field teach such diverse subjects as nutrition, child development, and family finances. Many others are involved in improving consumer products.

The Job

Family and consumer science is a broad field that employs people in diverse jobs and industries. Family and consumer scientists work in education, institution management, dietetics, research, social welfare, extension services, and business. Whatever the job, family and consumer scientists rely on their understanding of food and nutrition, child development, household management, and the many other elements involved in day-to-day living. For this article, the field has been divided into two areas: education and management/sales.

Education. Many family and consumer scientists teach in high schools and colleges. They instruct students on subjects such as foods, nutrition, textiles, clothing, child care and development, family relations, home furnishings and equipment, household economics, and home management. In addition, many metropolitan areas also offer adult education classes in skills such as tailoring, gourmet cooking, budgeting, and parenting. Many of these courses are taught by family and consumer scientists.

On the college level, family and consumer scientists teach courses that cover such subjects as the history of extension education, economics of aging, and nutrition education to prepare students for professional careers in the field. These professors also write articles and textbooks and conduct research.

Extension service family and consumer scientists are part of an educational system supported by the federal government, states, and counties to educate and advise families, both rural and urban, on family life, nutrition, child care, and other aspects of homemaking. These scientists offer help and advice over the phone and may also travel to various communities to give presentations and assistance.

Health and welfare agencies hire family and consumer scientists to collaborate with social workers, nurses, and physicians. They consult with low-income families who need help with financial management concerns. They develop community programs in health and nutrition, money management, and child care.

Family and consumer scientists are in demand in developing countries to advise government ministries, help in organizing schools, assist in the development of community projects, and work with people in other ways. The Peace Corps has a great need for family and consumer scientists, as do many other agencies.

Management/sales. The business world holds a wide range of opportunities for the family and consumer scientist. In general, most family and consumer scientists who work in business interpret consumers' needs to manufacturers, test and improve products and recipes, prepare booklets on product uses, plan educational programs and materials, and serve as a communications link between the consumer and the manufacturer. For example, a family and consumer scientist working in business might be hired by a food manufacturer to test and sample a variety of frozen pizzas made by other manufacturers and determine ways the company might improve its own frozen pizzas and become more competitive in the market.

Retail stores offer many jobs for the trained family and consumer scientist to help customers select home furnishings and equipment or to work in advertising, buying, fashion coordinating, and display. Many family and consumer scientists help consumers determine their needs and intentions when buying a product and then help them make the best choice.

Family and consumer scientists specializing in dietetics, nutrition, or institution management work in hospitals, hotels, restaurants, clubs, and schools planning nutritious, attractive meals for large numbers of people. They are concerned with ordering food and supervising its care, storage, and preparation; directing employees; handling budgets; and planning special diets, among other duties. The dietitian also may teach nutrition to student nurses, medical students, or dietetic interns. Community dietitians counsel groups or individuals on nutritional eating habits, nutrition on a budget, prevention of disease, and nutrition for older people and convalescents.

Family and consumer scientists who work in research create products and develop procedure to make life easier and better for consumers. Researchers are employed by colleges and universities, government agencies, industrial and commercial companies, and private agencies. For example, a consumer scientist might be hired by a food manufacturer to create a survey to determine people's opinions about frozen yogurt. After analyzing the survey results, the scientist can make recommendations about possible product changes or additions to the manufacturer of the frozen yogurt.

Requirements

HIGH SCHOOL

You should follow a college-preparatory program that includes courses in English, mathematics, science, foreign language, and government. Take any classes related to home economics, including family and consumer science, child development, adult living, and health. Take art classes—art skills will help you if you're working with children, in interior design, or in furniture sales.

POSTSECONDARY TRAINING

The minimum requirement for work as a family and consumer scientist is a bachelor's degree in family and consumer science or home economics. College teaching, research, and nutrition positions require master's or doctoral degrees in most cases. Many colleges and universities offer degrees in general family and consumer science, as well as specialization in subject areas of the field, including family and consumer science education, child development, foods and nutrition, dietetics, institution management, textiles and clothing, family economics and home management, household equipment and furnishings, and applied art. College work usually includes a core curriculum that gives the student an overview of the subject areas. In addition to family and consumer science subjects, a broad background in liberal arts and sciences is helpful.

CERTIFICATION OR LICENSING

For most business and sales positions, you won't need certification. To teach elementary or secondary school classes, you'll need to be licensed under regulations established by the department of education of your state. The American Association of Family and Consumer Sciences offers a voluntary certification program. To become certified, you must have at least a bachelor's degree and pass the National Family and Consumer Science Examination.

OTHER REQUIREMENTS

If teaching, patience is a virtue, as is organization. You'll need self-confidence in order to speak effectively before students of all ages. If working in the business sector, you should be ambitious and self-motivated.

Exploring

While it would seem that high school home economics courses would be the best opportunity to find out about family and consumer science as a profession, this is not always true. Many high school home economics courses are concerned with teaching homemaking skills to those whose education will end with high school. The high school home economics teacher can, however, provide useful information.

The community 4-H club offers a look at extension service work in action. You may be able to find a summer job in a family and consumer science-related activity, such as child care, clerking in a shop, or hospital kitchen work.

Employers

Those who teach family and consumer science can find work with public and private high schools, adult education programs, and consumer science college programs. Teachers also work for government extension programs. Those interested in business can find work with retail stores, supermarket chains, hotels, restaurants, food and appliance manufacturers, marketing companies, and research firms.

Starting Out

Most colleges and universities have placement centers to assist students and bring employers and graduates together. Many large firms go to campuses to interview prospective employees. Those interested in teaching should seek certification and apply to school districts. Many students work in the field of family and consumer science during college by participating in internships or summer employment. Often, these connections prove valuable in acquiring a permanent job, either at that organization or a related one.

In retail sales and product management, you may have to start at the bottom of the ladder with a company, in an entry-level position. With some experience, you'll be able to move on to assistant manager, then into management.

Advancement

In teaching and government work, there is usually a set pattern of advancement based on training and experience. Additional qualifications and experience lead to salary increases and better positions. College-level teachers can work toward tenure, then toward a promotion to full professor. In business, advancement occurs on the basis of skills, additional education, and dedication to your work.

Earnings

Earnings among family and consumer scientists vary a great deal, depending on experience, education, and area of work. Those in entry-level positions, such as salespeople and child care workers, may have annual earnings of well below $20,000. But teachers and those in upper-level sales and marketing jobs can earn considerably more. According to the *Occupational Outlook Handbook* (*OOH*), the median salary for elementary, middle, and secondary school teachers ranged from $37,610 to $42,080 in 2000. Home economics teachers in postsecondary institutions had median annual earnings of $46,500 in 2000, according to the U.S. Department of Labor. Salaries ranged from less than $23,960 to $84,320 or more per year. Food scientists earned an average of $52,160 a year in 2000, according to the *OOH*.

Benefits such as health insurance, vacation, and sick leave vary by employer. Family and consumer scientists who go into teaching will most certainly enjoy the usual fringe benefits of the profession, including paid sick leave, group insurance, and retirement plans, as well as having two to three months free each year for travel, further study, or other professional enrichment.

Work Environment

Family and consumer scientists generally work under pleasant conditions in any area of employment. Teachers often work extra hours assisting students and sponsoring home economics clubs, as well as teaching adult education classes, for which they are often paid extra. Extension workers, too, work long hours. Those in business and other areas generally work a 40-hour week. Family and consumer scientists who manage large facilities such as dining halls, school lunch programs, and hotel restaurants must be able to cope with the stress of overseeing a staff that prepares great amounts of food for large groups of people.

Outlook

The demand for family and consumer scientists will be highest for specialists in marketing, merchandising, family and consumer resource management, food service and institutional management, food science and human nutrition, environment and shelter, and textiles and clothing. Also, with the elderly population growing, family and consumer scientists will be actively involved in social services, gerontology, home health care, adult day services, and other programs that improve the quality of life for older people.

Those interested in teaching will find more opportunities at the elementary and secondary level than at the college level. As teachers, family and consumer science professionals will focus on preparing young people for better jobs and better lives. Vocational education programs, pregnancy prevention, and at-risk youth will be priorities for teachers and administrators.

For More Information

For a career brochure, Family and Consumer Sciences: Today's Profession Offering Tomorrow's Careers, *and information on certification, contact:*
AMERICAN ASSOCIATION OF FAMILY AND CONSUMER SCIENCES
1555 King Street
Alexandria, VA 22314
Tel: 703-706-4600
Email: info@aafcs.org
Web: http://www.aafcs.org

Farmers

Overview

Farmers either own or lease land on which they raise crops such as corn, wheat, tobacco, cotton, vegetables, or fruits; raise animals or poultry, mainly for food; or maintain herds of dairy cattle for the production of milk. Whereas some farmers may combine several of these activities, most specialize in one specific area. They are assisted by farm laborers—either hired workers or members of farm families—who perform various tasks.

As increasingly complex technology continues to impact the agricultural industry, farms are becoming larger. Most contemporary farms are thousands of acres in size and include massive animal and plant production operations. Subsistence farms that produce only enough to support the farmer's family are becoming increasingly rare. There are approximately 1.5 million farmers employed in the United States.

History

In colonial America, almost 95 percent of the population were farmers, planting such crops as corn, wheat, flax, and, further south, tobacco. Livestock including hogs, cattle, sheep, and goats were imported from Europe. Farmers raised hay to feed livestock and just enough other crops to supply their families with a balanced diet throughout the year. Progress in science and technology in the 18th and 19th centuries allowed for societies to develop in different directions, and to build other industries, but over one-half of the world's population is still engaged in farming today.

In the early 20th century, farmers raised a variety of crops along with cattle, poultry, and dairy cows. Farm labor was handled by the farmers and their families. Farmers were very self-sufficient, living on their farms and maintaining their own equipment and storage. Between 1910 and 1960, when horsepower was replaced by mechanized equipment, about 90 million acres previously devoted to growing hay for the feeding of horses could be planted with other crops. Advances in farming techniques and production led to larger farms and more specialization by farmers. Farmers began to focus on growing one or two crops. About this time, more tenant farmers entered the business, renting land for cash or share of the crops.

Farmers doubled their output between 1950 and 1980, but there were fewer of them. In that time, the farm population decreased from 23 million to 6 million. After 1980, farmers began supplementing their household income with off-farm jobs and businesses.

The Job

There are probably as many different types of farmers as there are different types of plants and animals whose products are consumed by humans. In addition to *diversified crops farmers,* who grow different combinations of fruits, grains, and vegetables, and *general farmers,* who raise livestock as well as crops, there are *cash grain farmers,* who grow barley, corn, rice, soybeans, and wheat; *vegetable farmers; tree-fruit-and-nut crops farmers; field crops farmers,* who raise alfalfa, cotton, hops, peanuts, mint, sugarcane, and tobacco; *animal breeders; fur farmers; livestock ranchers; dairy farmers; poultry farmers; beekeepers; reptile farmers; fish farmers;* and even *worm growers.*

In addition to the different types of crop farmers, there are two different types of farming management careers: the farm operator and the farm manager.

The *farm operator* either owns his or her own farm or leases land from other farms. Farm operators' responsibilities vary depending on the type of farm they run, but in general they are responsible for making managerial decisions. They determine the best time to seed, fertilize, cultivate, spray, and harvest. They keep extensive financial and inventory records of the farm operations, which are now done with the help of computer programs.

Farm operators perform tasks ranging from caring for livestock to erecting sheds. The size of the farm often determines what tasks the operators handle themselves. On very large farms, operators hire employees to perform tasks that operators on small farms would do themselves.

The *farm manager* has a wide range of duties. The owner of a large livestock farm may hire a farm manager to oversee a single activity, such as feeding the livestock. In other cases, a farm manager may oversee the entire operation of a small farm for an absentee owner. Farm management firms often employ highly skilled farm managers to manage specific operations on a small farm or to oversee tenant farm operations on several farms.

Whether farm operators or managers, the farmers' duties vary widely depending on what product they farm. A common type of farmer is the *crop farmer*. Following are a number of crops that a crop farmer might manage.

Corn farmers and wheat farmers begin the growing season by breaking up the soil with plows, then harrowing, pulverizing, and leveling it. Some of these tasks may be done after the harvest the previous year and others just before planting. Corn is usually planted around the middle of May with machines that place the corn seeds into dirt hills a few inches apart, making weed control easier. On the average, a crop is cultivated three times during a season. Corn is also used in the making of silage, a type of animal feed made by cutting the corn and allowing it to ferment in storage silos.

Wheat may be sown in the fall or spring, depending on the severity of the past winter and the variety of wheat being sown. Wheat is planted with a drill, close together, allowing greater cultivation and easier harvesting. The harvest for winter wheat occurs in early summer. Wheat farmers use combines to gather and thresh the wheat in one operation. The wheat is then stored in large grain storage elevators, which are owned by private individuals, companies, or farming cooperatives.

Cotton and tobacco planting begins in March in the Southwest and somewhat later in the Southeast. Tobacco plants must be carefully protected from harsh weather conditions. The soil in which tobacco is grown must be thoroughly broken up, smoothed, and fertilized before planting, as tobacco is very hard on the soil.

The peanut crop can be managed like other types of farm crops. It is not especially sensitive to weather and disease, nor does it require the great care of tobacco and cotton.

Specialty crops such as fruits and vegetables are subject to seasonal variations, so the farmer usually relies heavily on hired seasonal labor. This type of farmer uses more specialized equipment than do general farmers.

The mechanization of farming has not eliminated all the problems of raising crops. Judgment and experience are always important in making decisions. The hay farmer, for example, must determine the time for mowing that will yield the best crop in terms of stem toughness and leaf loss. These decisions must be weighed against possible harsh weather conditions. To harvest hay, hay farmers use specialized equipment such as mowing machines and hay rakes that are usually drawn by tractors. The hay is pressed into bales by another machine for easier storage and then transported to storage facilities or to market.

Decisions about planting are just as crucial as those about harvesting. For example, potatoes need to be planted during a relatively short span of days in the spring. The fields must be tilled and ready for planting, and the farmer must estimate weather conditions so the seedlings will not freeze from late winter weather.

The crop specialty farmer uses elaborate irrigation systems to water crops during seasons of inadequate rainfall. Often these systems are portable as it is necessary to move the equipment from field to field.

Farms are strongly influenced by the weather, diseases, fluctuations in prices of domestic and foreign farm products, and, in some cases, federal farm programs. Farmers must carefully plan the combination of crops they will grow so that if the price of one crop drops they will have sufficient income from another to make up for it. Since prices change from month to month, farmers who plan ahead may be able to store their crops or keep their livestock to take advantage of better prices later in the year.

Farmers who raise and breed animals for milk or meat are called livestock and cattle farmers. There are various types of farmers that fall into this category.

Livestock farmers generally buy calves from ranchers who breed and raise them. They feed and fatten young cattle and often raise their own corn and hay to lower feeding costs. They need to be familiar with cattle diseases and proper methods of feeding. They provide their cattle with fenced pasturage and adequate shelter from rough weather. Some livestock farmers specialize in breeding stock for sale to ranchers and dairy farmers. These specialists maintain and improve purebred animals of a particular breed. Bulls and cows are then sold to ranchers and dairy farmers who want to improve their herds.

Sheep ranchers raise sheep primarily for their wool. Large herds are maintained on rangeland in the western states. Since large areas of land are needed, the sheep rancher must usually buy grazing rights on government-owned lands.

Although the *dairy farmers'* first concern is the production of high-grade milk, they also raise corn and grain to provide feed for their animals. Dairy farmers must be able to repair the many kinds of equipment essential to their business and know about diseases, sanitation, and methods of improving the quantity and quality of the milk.

Dairy animals must be milked twice every day, once in the morning and once at night. Records are kept of each cow's production of milk to ascertain which cows are profitable and which should be traded or sold for meat. After milking, when the cows are at pasture, the farmer cleans the stalls and barn by washing, sweeping, and sterilizing milking equipment with boiling water. This is extremely important because dairy cows easily contract diseases from unsanitary conditions, and this in turn may contaminate the milk. Dairy farmers must have their herds certified to be free of disease by the U.S. Department of Health.

The great majority of *poultry farmers* do not hatch their own chicks but buy them from commercial hatcheries. The chicks are kept in brooder houses until they are seven or eight weeks old and are then transferred to open pens or shelters. After six months, the hens begin to lay eggs and roosters are culled from the flock to be sold for meat.

The primary duty of poultry farmers is to keep their flocks healthy. They provide shelter from the chickens' natural enemies and from extreme weather conditions. The shelters are kept extremely clean, because diseases can spread through a flock rapidly. The poultry farmer selects the food that best allows each chicken to grow or produce to its greatest potential while at the same time keeping costs down.

Raising chickens to be sold as broilers or fryers requires equipment to house them until they are six to 13 weeks old. Farmers specializing in the production of eggs gather eggs at least twice a day and more often in very warm weather. The eggs are stored in a cool place, inspected, graded, and packed for market. The poultry farmer who specializes in producing broilers is usually not an independent producer but is under contract with a backer, who is often the operator of a slaughterhouse or the manufacturer of poultry feeds.

Beekeepers set up and manage bee hives and harvest and sell the excess honey that bees don't use as their own food. The sale of honey is less profitable than the business of cultivating bees for lease to farmers to help pollinate their crops.

Farmers and farm managers make a wide range of administrative decisions. In addition to their knowledge of crop production and animal science, they determine how to market the foods they produce. They keep an eye on the commodities markets to see which crops are most profitable. They take out loans to buy farm equipment or additional land for cultivation. They keep up with new methods of production and new markets. Farms today are large, complex businesses, complete with the requisite anxiety over cash flow, competition, markets, and production.

Requirements

HIGH SCHOOL
Take classes in math, accounting, and business to prepare for the management responsibilities of running a farm. To further assist you in management, take computer classes. Chemistry, biology, and earth science classes can help you understand the various processes of crop production. Technical and shop courses will help you to better understand agricultural machinery. With county extension courses, you can keep abreast of developments in farm technology.

POSTSECONDARY TRAINING
Although there are no specific educational requirements for this field, every successful farmer, whether working with crops or ani-

mals, must have a knowledge of the principles of soil preparation and cultivation, disease control, and machinery maintenance, as well as a mastery of business practices and bookkeeping. Farmers must know their crops well enough to be able to choose the proper seeds for their particular soil and climate. They also need experience in evaluating crop growth and weather cycles. Livestock and dairy farmers should enjoy working with animals and have some background in animal science, breeding, and care.

The state land-grant universities across the country were established to encourage agricultural research and to educate young people in the latest advancements in farming. They offer agricultural programs that award bachelor's degrees as well as shorter programs in specific areas. Some universities offer advanced studies in horticulture, animal science, agronomy, and agricultural economics. Most students in agricultural colleges are also required to take courses in farm management, business, finance, and economics. Two-year colleges often have programs leading to associate degrees in agriculture.

CERTIFICATION OR LICENSING

The American Society of Farm Managers and Rural Appraisers offers farm operators voluntary certification as an accredited farm manager (AFM). Certification requires several years experience working on a farm, an academic background—a bachelor's or preferably a master's degree in a branch of agricultural science—and courses covering the business, financial, and legal aspects of farm management.

OTHER REQUIREMENTS

You'll need to keep up to date on new farming methods throughout the world. You must be flexible and innovative enough to adapt to new technologies that will produce crops or raise livestock more efficiently. You should also have good mechanical aptitude and be able to work with a wide variety of tools and machinery.

Exploring

Most people who become farmers have grown up on farms; if your family doesn't own a farm, there are opportunities for part-time work as a hired hand, especially during seasonal operations. If you live in an agricultural community, you should be able to find work as a detasseler in the summer time. Although the work is hot and strenuous, it will quickly familiarize you with aspects of crop production and the hard work it takes to operate a farm.

Oganizations such as 4-H (http://www.fourhcouncil.edu) and the National FFA Organization (http://www.ffa.org) offer good opportunities for learning about, visiting, and participating in farming activities. Agricultural colleges often have their own farms where students can gain actual experience in farm operations in addition to classroom work.

Employers

Farmers are self-employed, working on land they've inherited, purchased, or leased. Those who don't own land, but who have farming experience, may find work on large commercial farms or with agricultural supply companies as consultants or managers. Farmers with seasonal crops may work for agriculture-related businesses during the off-season or may work temporarily as farm hands for livestock farms and ranches. They may also own other businesses, such as farm equipment sales and service.

Starting Out

It is becoming increasingly difficult for a person to purchase land for farming. The capital investment in a farm today is so great that it is almost impossible for anyone to start from scratch. However, those who lack a family connection to farming or who do not have enough money to start their own farm can lease land from other farmers. Money for leasing land and equipment may be available from local banks or the Farmers Home Administration.

Because the capital outlay is so high, many wheat, corn, and specialty crop farmers often start as tenant farmers, renting land and equipment. They may also share the cash profits with the owner of the land. In this way, these tenants hope to gain both the experience and cash to purchase and manage their own farms.

Livestock farmers generally start by renting property and sometimes animals on a share-of-the-profits basis with the owner. Government lands, such as national parks, can be rented for pasture as well. Later, when the livestock farmer wants to own property, it is possible to borrow based on the estimated value of the leased land, buildings, and animals. Dairy farmers can begin in much the same way. However, loans are becoming more difficult to obtain. After several years of lenient loan policies, financial institutions in farm regions have tightened their requirements.

Advancement

Farmers advance by buying their own farms or additional acreage to increase production and income. With a farm's success, a farmer can also invest in better equipment and technology and can hire managers and workers to attend to much of the farm's operation. This is true for crop, livestock, dairy, or poultry farmers. In farming, as in other fields, a person's success depends greatly on education, motivation, and keeping up with the latest developments.

Earnings

Farmers' incomes vary greatly from year to year, since the prices of farm products fluctuate according to weather conditions and the amount and quality of what all farmers were able to produce. A farm that shows a large profit one year may show a loss for the following year. Most farmers, especially those running small farms, earn incomes from nonfarm activities that are several times larger than their farm incomes. Farm incomes also vary greatly depending on the size and type of farm. In general, large farms generate more income than small farms. Exceptions include some specialty farms that produce low-volume but high-quality horticultural and fruit products.

The Economic Research Service (ERS) of the U.S. Department of Agriculture reports there are currently slightly more than 2.1 million farm households in the country. The ERS forecast the average farm household income to be $62,021 in 2001. This income, it is important to note, includes earnings from off-farm jobs, businesses, and other sources.

In addition to size and type of farm, location is also an important factor in farm incomes. According to Agricultural Resource Management Survey findings, the average 2000 household income (including off-farm sources) was $57,525 for farms in the Heartland region. Also in 2000, farms in the Mississippi Portal region had an average household income of $46,174, while the highest average household income of $82,129 was reported from the Fruitful Rim Region.

Farm managers who worked full-time had median weekly earnings of $542 in 2000 (or approximately $28,185 per year), according to the *Occupational Outlook Handbook.* The lowest paid 10 percent of farm managers earned less than $187 weekly, and the top 10 percent of all farm managers earned $756 or more per week.

Work Environment

The farmer's daily life has its rewards and dangers. Machine-related injuries, exposure to the weather, and illnesses caused by allergies or animal-related diseases are just some of the hazards that farmers face on a regular basis. In addition, farms are often isolated, away from many conveniences and necessities such as immediate medical attention.

Farming can be a difficult and frustrating career, but for many it is a satisfying way of life. The hours are long and the work is physically strenuous, but working outdoors and watching the fruits of one's labor grow before one's eyes can be very rewarding. The changing seasons bring variety to the day-to-day work. Farmers seldom work five eight-hour days a week. When harvesting time comes or the weather is right for planting or spraying, farmers work long hours to see that everything gets done. Even during the cold winter months they stay busy repairing machinery and buildings. Dairy farmers and other livestock farmers work seven days a week all year round.

Outlook

The *Occupational Outlook Handbook* predicts that employment of farmers and ranchers is expected to decline through 2010. The department predicts that employment for farm and ranch managers will grow more slowly than the average during that same time span. Every year can be different for farmers, as production, expansion, and markets are affected by weather, exports, and other factors. Land prices are expected to drop some, but so are the prices for grain, hogs, and cattle. Throughout the 20th century, the U.S. government was active in aiding farmers, but in recent years has attempted to step back from agricultural production. But the state of farming today is calling for more government involvement. Some trends that farmers may follow in their efforts to increase income include more diversified crop production; for example, farmers may choose to plant high-oil or high-protein corn, which bring more money in the marketplace. But these new grains also require different methods of storage and marketing.

Large corporate farms are fast replacing the small farmer, who is being forced out of the industry by the spiraling costs of feed, grain, land, and equipment. The late 1970s and early 1980s were an especially hard time for farmers. Many small farmers were forced to give up farming; some lost farms that had been in their families for generations. Some small-scale farmers, however, have found opportunities in organic food production, farmers' markets, and similar market niches that require more direct personal contact with their customers.

Despite the great difficulty in becoming a farmer today, there are many agriculture-related careers that involve people with farm production, marketing, management, and agribusiness.

For More Information

For more farming information, contact the following:
AMERICAN FARM BUREAU FEDERATION
225 Touhy Avenue
Park Ridge, IL 60068
Web: http://www.fb.org

NATIONAL COUNCIL OF FARMER COOPERATIVES
50 F Street, NW, Suite 900
Washington, DC 20001
Tel: 202-626-8700
Web: http://www.ncfc.org

U.S. DEPARTMENT OF AGRICULTURE
Washington, DC 20250
Tel: 202-720-2791
Web: http://www.usda.gov

Fast Food Workers

Overview

Whether the restaurant's menu lists pizza, tacos, hamburgers, or fried chicken, a *fast food worker* is responsible for serving each customer the correct order in an efficient, professional, and courteous manner. Fast food workers may work in large chain restaurants or privately owned shops. Most of these places serve only one kind of food, but some establishments have a wide selection of dishes. In either type of restaurant, fast food workers need to be familiar with the menu, including prices, portion sizes, side dishes, and how the food is prepared.

History

The continual development of new transportation methods throughout history has made travel easier. While away from their homes and kitchens, travelers needed places to eat. As a result, concepts in alternative dining facilities have multiplied. Early travelers would eat meals at hotels, inns, and taverns in towns. When train layovers began to allow for meal breaks, food carts offering stews and quick dinners soon appeared near train depots. Longer, scheduled train stops provided passengers with the opportunity to enjoy a more leisurely meal at local inns and diners.

After the turn of the century, train travel in the United States became more popular and efficient. Passengers commonly took much longer trips from state to state. At the same time, trains offered travelers reasonably priced meals in dining cars. When automobile travel became popular, small independent stands were built along roadsides, offering hurried travelers meals and sandwiches that were prepared and served quickly. With the development of highways and freeways, roadside restaurants began to thrive.

Today, many well-known fast food franchises can be found both in metropolitan areas and along highways throughout the United States. Many American restaurant chains have established themselves in countries around the world. The most famous is probably McDonald's, the third-oldest food service restaurant chain in the United States.

In 1930, fried chicken was the specialty in a small Kentucky restaurant opened by a man named Colonel Sanders. By 1956, Sanders was promoting his own recipe throughout the area, and eventually his one-restaurant business became the famous Kentucky Fried Chicken, now known worldwide. The second-oldest fast food chain is Burger King, which was opened by the Burger King Corporation of Miami, Florida, in 1954.

Fast food has become increasingly popular because it fits into the busy schedules of most working families. In addition, restaurants are conveniently located, offer moderately priced meals, and serve a consistent, dependable food product. Many fast food restaurants offer price specials or discounts, such as "two-for-one" deals. Responding to the widespread interest in more healthy lifestyles, some restaurants are supplementing their menus with food such as salads, soups, and low-fat items.

The Job

Fast food workers may have a variety of duties. Some fast food establishments require employees to be familiar with all aspects of the restaurant: greeting and serving customers, cleanup and maintenance, and preparation of some of the simpler food items. Larger chain restaurants may institute this practice as a way of familiarizing the fast food worker with the restaurant's needs as a whole, with the possibility of specialization later. Smaller restaurants, not having enough staff to allow specialization, may follow this pattern out of necessity.

Fast food workers who are part of the kitchen staff may begin as assistants to the trained cooks. These assistants may help set up supplies, refill condiment containers, or do prep work such as slicing meats or vegetables. These assistants also may be responsible for general cleanup duties in the kitchen area.

Kitchen staff employees who cook are responsible for preparing all food to meet the company's standards. In this regard, the food must be made consistently and neatly.

The *cashier* in a fast food restaurant is responsible for taking the customer's order, entering the order into the computer or cash register, taking payment, and returning proper change. In some fast food establishments the cashier may act as *counter worker* and have additional tasks. These added duties can include filling the customer's order and serving it to the customer on a tray or in a carryout container. It is often the cashier's duty to greet customers, welcoming them to the restaurant in a friendly and courteous way.

In addition to interacting with the customers, the counter worker must also be able to communicate effectively with the kitchen and managerial staff. The counter worker may have to tell the kitchen staff about a special order for a sandwich or shortages of certain food items. The counter worker may need to notify the manager about a problem with the register or a disgruntled customer. Since delays can take away from customer satisfaction and hurt the restaurant's business, the counter worker has to identify, communicate, and solve problems quickly.

Good fast food employees learn to work under pressure and meet the work standards that their managers expect. A fast food worker also learns tangible skills, such as working a cash register, cooking, and communicating. In the different areas of fast food work, employees must be able to keep up the pace, show personal motivation, and be willing to work as part of a team.

Unlike some other types of work, however, the fast food business is a no-nonsense job. A cashier or counter worker may handle hundreds of dollars a day. Cooks work over fryers and grills and handle knives and meat slicers. The work requires concentration and a professional attitude.

Requirements

HIGH SCHOOL
Students who are working part-time jobs and are still in high school may find that courses such as home economics, advanced

cooking, or health and sanitation may be helpful. As fast food workers make their way up the ranks of the restaurant, they may decide to pursue special training or education.

POSTSECONDARY TRAINING
If a fast food employee is already working full-time at a large franchise and is interested in pursuing management training, there are many outlets for career preparation. Many franchises have their own training programs for future managers and franchise owners. McDonald's, Dunkin' Donuts, and Burger King all offer serious course work in such areas as maintaining restaurant equipment; hiring, training, and motivating employees; and purchasing supplies. Most other chain franchises offer employee instruction as well, so that the product and image of their restaurants are kept consistent and so that they may offer new franchise owners assistance in getting started in the business.

OTHER REQUIREMENTS
For an entry-level position at a fast food restaurant, a worker should be motivated, cheerful, and cooperative. The fast food business requires a quick pace, especially during rush periods. A motivated employee is willing to work extra hard and offer help to a fellow employee during these times. When the restaurant is busy, paying close attention and thinking quickly are as necessary in accepting money and counting back change as they are in the handling of food.

Fast food workers should be neat in appearance as well as have good work habits. Some fast food restaurants require that their employees wear uniforms or follow a dress code. They also may dictate specific rules of behavior. Because such guidelines are important for both safety reasons and the atmosphere of the restaurant, employees must respect and follow them. Failure to do so may result in the employee being sent home or having his or her pay reduced. The good qualities and work habits that are found in reliable fast food workers reflect the professional attitude that managers and franchise owners strive for in their restaurants.

Exploring

Course work in home economics and other classes that develop cooking skills can provide good preparation for the job of a fast food worker. In addition, general business or management courses provide a solid basis for entry-level workers. Students should also look into opportunities for working in the school cafeteria or other food service area. Neighborhood restaurants and local hot dog or hamburger stands may also hire summer help.

Certain high schools offer cooperative work-study programs to students to assist them in gaining job experience. Such programs may offer concentrations in the food service industry.

Employers

Fast food workers may be employed by large chain restaurants or privately owned shops.

Starting Out

At some fast food restaurants, more than 50 percent of the positions are for part-time employees. Applying at restaurants that hire part-time or student help is a good way to enter this field. Even at smaller, privately owned establishments, the fast food worker will be introduced to some of the common factors of the industry: working with and for a variety of people, keeping up a quick pace, and cooking, packaging, and serving food in a friendly way.

Local papers often advertise for help in neighborhood restaurants, and some fast food establishments contact school counseling departments to post job openings. The majority of positions are available to those who walk in and fill out an application. Since entry-level positions open up and are filled quickly, applicants are advised to contact restaurants regularly if no openings are immediately available.

Advancement

Because of the diversity in the restaurant business, there is ample opportunity for workers to find an area of interest or specialization. Fast food workers may take advantage of manager-trainee opportunities or tuition assistance to move higher up within the company. Some fast food workers use their experience to go on to other areas of food service, such as waiting tables or working as a restaurant host or manager. Others may decide to go to a vocational cooking school or pursue hotel and restaurant management careers.

Earnings

Like other entry-level workers with part-time jobs, fast food workers can expect to begin at the minimum hourly wage—$5.15. Hourly salaries for fast food cooks ranged from $5.49 and $8.43 in 2000, according to the *Occupational Outlook Handbook.* The median hourly salary for fast food cooks was $6.53 in 2000. Full-time food preparation workers earned average hourly salaries of $7.38 per week in 2000. Some food preparation workers earned over $10.65 per hour, while the lowest full-time workers earned $5.67 or less per hour.

Larger restaurant franchises often offer annual and bonus raises. Restaurants that have late evening or all-night hours may compensate employees working those shifts with higher hourly wages. Sometimes employees earn additional compensation or time-and-a-half for working overtime or on holidays. Some restaurants and individually owned franchises offer bonuses for tuition assistance, as well as periodic bonuses.

Work Environment

Fast food restaurants need to meet the safety and sanitary standards enforced by local and state health departments. These agencies require an establishment to have proper lighting and adequate heating, cooling, and ventilation systems so employees can work in a comfortable environment.

Large fast food franchises are often decorated pleasantly, incorporating the logo, color schemes, or trademark characters of their parent companies. They supply adequate and comfortable seating facilities, which are maintained according to corporate standards.

Fast food employees may work shifts of five to nine hours and receive appropriate coffee and lunch breaks. These establishments often have private rooms, separated from the main dining rooms, for employees to eat lunches and relax.

Fast food workers may have regular work hours (mornings only, for example) or floating schedules that require them to work a combination of evenings, afternoons, and weekends. Fast food workers may be called in by their managers to work an extra shift or work overtime if another employee is ill or if the restaurant is very busy. Fast food workers should be fairly flexible because their managers have no way to determine in advance how busy or under-staffed the restaurant will be.

Outlook

More Americans are choosing to eat at full-service restaurants, which should limit employment growth for fast food workers, espe-cially cooks. Despite this trend, job opportunities for all types of food and beverage workers are expected to be plentiful for the next decade or more. Most openings will result from a need to replace workers who have left the field for other professions.

Entry-level jobs are not difficult to come by. Submitting an application and keeping in touch with managers for openings can lead to the beginning of a successful career in the fast food indus-try. Owning a franchise is a popular business venture, but one that demands the recruitment and promotion of reliable, capable staff. Knowledge of the business from the bottom up is a definite advan-tage for franchise owners.

For More Information

This trade association offers information on food service employ-ee requirements and training.
NATIONAL RESTAURANT ASSOCIATION EDUCATIONAL FOUNDATION
250 South Wacker Drive, Suite 1400
Chicago, IL 60606
Tel: 312-715-1010
Web: http://www.edfound.org

Fishers

Quick Facts

School Subjects
Business
Technical/shop

Personal Skills
Following instructions
Mechanical/manipulative

Work Environment
Primarily outdoors
Primarily multiple locations

Minimum Education Level
High school diploma

Salary Range
$15,600 to $27,300 to $39,000

Certification or Licensing
None available

Outlook
Decline

Overview

Fishers catch fish and other marine life by net, trap, and hook and then sell their catch to commercial food processors, restaurants, and fish markets. Fishers work both in the ocean and fresh water bodies. Some fishers run recreational charter fishing businesses: they rent power boats, provide fishing expertise, and take customers out on the water for sport fishing trips. The U.S. Bureau of Labor Statistics estimates that fishers and fishing vessel operators hold over 53,000 jobs, with about six out of 10 of these workers self-employed.

History

When Europeans began to colonize North America, commercial fishing became a major industry. At that time, America enjoyed a great abundance of fish and other marine life. The continent's lakes and streams teemed with trout and perch. The Gulf of Mexico offered up shrimp and oysters. In Pacific waters swam tuna and salmon, and the Atlantic Ocean shore was crowded with lobster and crab. Fleets of fishing boats and mammoth whaling ships headed out to sea, returning with huge catches. For many communities, fishing was the dominant way of life. Grueling and dangerous, but also rugged and exciting, fishing held and still holds charm and excitement for those who want to work under the open sky.

Time has changed the fishing industry drastically. Pollution has made many waters unfishable. Increasing government regulation keeps fishers from catching as they did in the past. In addition, technological advances have changed how people look for, catch, and process fish. The family fishing boat has given way to the corporate fishing fleet. But some of the old romance about fishing lingers, and the occupation still attracts a steady stream of workers.

The Job

Now that large corporate fishing fleets dominate the fishing industry, most fishing is done from large commercial vessels that employ many fishers as crew. The *captain* plans and oversees the entire fishing operation. He or she decides which fish should be caught, where they will best be found, the method of capture, the duration of the trip, and how the catch will be sold. The captain also makes sure the sailing vessel is in suitable condition and hires and supervises crew members. The *first mate* is the captain's assistant. He or she must be familiar with navigation requirements and up to date on all the latest electronic devices used on fishing boats. The mate, under the supervision of the captain, oversees the fishing operations and the sailing responsibilities of the *deckhands*. The *boatswain* is an experienced deckhand with some supervisory responsibilities. He or she directs the loading of equipment and supplies onto the vessel before it sets sail. The boatswain also operates and repairs much of the fishing gear. The deckhands do much of the actual fishing. Deckhands release and pull in nets and lines and extract the catch from the lines or nets. They wash, salt, ice, and store the fish. Deckhands also make sure that the deck is clean and clear at all times and that the vessel's engines and equipment are in working order.

Fishers are classified according to the type of equipment they use, the type of fish they catch, and where they go to catch them. Fishers work all over the country. Major fishing industries can be found in Maine, Maryland, Massachusetts, Louisiana, Florida, Texas, California, Oregon, Washington, and Alaska. The northeastern states are good for lobster and sardine fishing, while fishers in the Gulf states catch shrimp and oysters. Most tuna fishers work off the California coastline. U.S. vessels also travel into the

Bering Sea for snow crab, halibut, pollock, and salmon and to the oceans off Africa and China for tuna.

Net fishers are usually deep sea fishers. They either work alone or as part of a crew, using many types of nets to catch fish. Some boats make only short day runs, while others go for weeks or months at a time, keeping their catches fresh in huge refrigeration units. While small boats may carry a few crew members, large tuna boats can carry as many as 22 and measure more than 200 feet long.

After the boats leave port, they head for the areas of the sea that are known to have fish. Crew members keep track of weather reports and fishing conditions over the radio. They scan for schools of fish using sonar and other electronic equipment. When they think they have located a school of fish, they lower the nets. *Purse seiners,* who mainly catch tuna, use a huge net—often a mile long and hundreds of feet deep. The net is weighted on the bottom and is held vertical by floats attached to the top. A smaller boat called a skiff, driven by a skiff operator, holds one end of the net while the fishing vessel circles around the school to surround it with the net. Once that is done, fishers close the bottom of the net by retracting steel cables that act like a drawstring, then pull in the net and haul the catch on board.

Net fishers are responsible for readying and repairing nets while the boat is moving to and from the fishing waters. The catch is often so heavy that they must use hydraulic pumps and conveyor belts to haul it in. Depending on the captain's orders, fish may be cleaned and sorted before or after returning to shore. Large tuna boats that stay at sea for many weeks catch as many as 1,200 tons of fish, which the fishers usually turn over to canneries upon their return.

Line fishers catch fish with poles, hooks, and lines. They work alone or in crews. They lay out lines and attach hooks, bait, and other equipment, depending on the type of fish they plan to catch. This process can take several hours. They then lower these lines into the water. To haul catches on board they use reels, winches, or their bare hands. They take the fish off the hooks, sometimes stunning them first by hitting them with clubs. They store their catch in the boat's hold or in boxes packed with ice. Some of these fishers use a gaff—a long pole with a hook on the end—to help them catch fish and bring them aboard. Line fishers may also clean fish while their vessel heads to shore.

Because ships usually do not return to shore until bad weather, darkness, or the ship's hold is full of fish, net and line fishers will repeat their tasks several times a day.

Pot fishers trap crab, eel, and lobster using baited cages with funnel-shaped net openings. They fish near the shore or in inland waters off small boats. Pot fishing is done by lowering the cages into the water, pulling them in when the fish are trapped, and dumping the catch onto the deck. These fishers must measure each animal to make sure it is large enough to lawfully keep. Undersize fish are thrown back into the water. When catching lobster, fishers must sometimes insert pegs between the hinges of their claws to keep them from killing each other in the hold of the ship. Pot fishers often sell their catches live to processors who can, freeze, or sell them fresh. Because they are hardy animals, lobster and crab are often sold and shipped to various places while they are still alive.

Terrapin fishers trap terrapin turtles by stretching nets across marshes, creeks, or rivers and chasing the terrapins into the nets. They may pole a skiff around in grassy waters and catch terrapins with a hand net or wade in mud and catch them by hand. *Weir fishers* make traps out of brush or netting, chase the fish into them, and remove the catch with a purse seine or net. *Oyster fishers* harvest oysters from beds in bays or river estuaries, using tongs, grabs, and dredges. They create "sea farms" to grow their catches by creating an environment suitable for growing oysters and keeping natural predators out of the oysters' waters.

While most fishers are involved with commercial fishing, some captains and deckhands are primarily involved with recreational fishing. Typically a group of people charter a fishing vessel—for periods ranging from several hours to a few days—for sport fishing, socializing, and relaxation. The captain and crew are responsible for a safe voyage and will usually help the recreational fishers on board with their fishing.

Requirements

HIGH SCHOOL
There probably aren't many classes offered at your high school that will involve you directly with fishing and boats, especially if you live far from the water. But there are courses that can give you back-

ground on the career. Geography and history will teach you about the climates and industry of various fishing villages and port cities around the world; in biology class, you'll learn something about marine life. Agriculture courses may also include units in the fishing industry. Take shop courses, as you may be required to repair your fishing machinery. Business courses will prepare you for record-keeping and accounting details of self-employment.

POSTSECONDARY TRAINING
Fishers learn their skills through experience on the job. Certain academic courses, however, can help prepare workers for their first job. Some high schools, colleges, and technical schools in port cities offer useful courses in handling boats and fishing equipment, biology, meteorology, navigation, and marketing. Associate degree and certificate programs in fishery technologies, commercial fishing, and aquaculture are also available at some community colleges, such as Bellingham Technical College, Washington (http://www.beltc.ctc.edu); Mt. Hood Community College, Oregon (http://www.mhcc.cc.or.us); Clatsop Community College, Oregon (http://www.clatsopcollege.com); and Morrisville State University of New York, New York (http://www.morrisville.edu). Some four year schools also offer related bachelor's degrees; for example, the University of Rhode Island offers a bachelor's degree in environment and life science in which students can concentrate on aquaculture and fisheries technology (http://www.uri.edu). These programs usually combine course work and hands-on experience in the fishing industry.

Experienced fishers often take short-term courses offered by postsecondary schools. These programs provide information on electronic navigation and communications equipment and the latest improvements in fishing gear.

CERTIFICATION OR LICENSING
Captains and first mates on large fishing vessels of at least 200 gross tons must be licensed. Captains of charter sport fishing boats must also be licensed, regardless of the size of the vessel. Crew members on certain fish processing vessels may require merchant mariner's documentation. These licenses and documents are issued by the U.S. Coast Guard. Individuals seeking certification must meet physical and academic requirements.

OTHER REQUIREMENTS

People who enjoy risk, independence, and hard work may enjoy commercial fishing. Fishers should be self-sufficient and able to cope with the everyday dangers of working with heavy equipment on wet decks and in stormy seas. Teamwork is essential when seas become rough or equipment breaks down, so fishers must stay calm in the face of trouble. Mechanical aptitude is also essential as fishers spend a good deal of time setting up, repairing, and maintaining equipment. Business acumen will help those fishers who want to be skippers of their own boats.

Exploring

If you live on one of the coasts, you can try to find summer work on a small fishing boat or at a fishing port. You might at least have the opportunity to go out on a fishing boat; contact a state department of fish and game to learn more about the local fishing industry, and about opportunities to meet fishers. If you don't live near the water, you can learn about salt water fish by working for a pet shop or a state aquarium.

After high school, you can look into working for a cold storage facility or cannery in Alaska. Though this factory-line work, called working on the "slime line," won't involve actually going out in a fishing boat, you will get a great sense of the business, and will have the opportunity to meet people in the commercial fishing industry.

Employers

States along the coast, such as Alaska, California, and Maine, have large fishing industries. Fishers either work for a family-run operation, or a large cannery that has its own commercial vessels. Fishing crews are generally small, with only a few people attending to all the various details, from running the boat to setting up the equipment, and hauling in the fish. Fishers may also find work with a crew that only accompanies sporting expeditions; in such cases, they are involved in escorting recreational fishing teams out to sea for a few days.

Starting Out

To work as a fisher, you'll have to hire on with one of the fishing boats along the coasts. These fishing operations are often family-based, or work with the same crew of seasoned veterans every year. Without connections, you may be able to find a job with a fishing crew if you happen to be in the right place at the right time. You can seek a deckhand's job with a captain, or take a job with a cannery, in order to gain some experience with the industry.

You could start your own fishing business, but it would be very costly. Some vessels cost around $350,000 to buy, and millions to build. These vessels also require tens of thousands of dollars to operate every year. You may also have to buy a permit to have access to a fishery; the price of these permits can be as high as $450,000. Loans for boats and permits may be available from the U.S. Small Business Administration, or from the state's department of commerce.

Advancement

Fishing has little formal structure within which workers can advance. Fishers can, however, increase their earnings and responsibilities by becoming more skilled at vessel and net operation and more involved in all aspects of the fishing industry. Enterprising fishers who save enough money may be able to buy their own boats. Some run their own processing operations or catch seafood for their own restaurants. Advancement is limited only by the individual's own desire, drive, and skill. Owning one boat or a number of boats usually provides the highest profits for commercial fishers.

Earnings

Earnings of fishers vary with the season, economy, abundance of fish, market demands, and workers' skills and willingness to stay out at sea. Few fishers receive a fixed wage. Instead, they usually earn percentages of the catch's receipts. In New England, ship owners can receive 50 percent of the catch's receipts. The captain may receive 10 percent, and the crew share the remaining 40 percent. According to the Alaska Department of Fish and Game, a crew

Food Service Workers

Overview

Food service workers include waiters (the term waiter refers to both male and female servers), counter attendants, dining room attendants, hosts, fast food workers, kitchen assistants, and others. These workers take customers' orders, serve food and beverages, make out customers' checks, and sometimes take payments. These basic duties, however, may vary greatly depending on the specific kind of food service establishment. There are approximately 5.6 million people working as waiters, helpers, attendants, hosts, and other food servers in the United States.

Quick Facts

School Subjects
  Family and consumer science
  Mathematics
Personal Skills
  Following instructions
  Helping/teaching
Work Environment
  Primarily indoors
  Primarily one location
Minimum Education Level
  High school diploma
Salary Range
  $4,430 to $13,580 to $21,110+
  (plus tips)
Certification or Licensing
  Required by all states
Outlook
  About as fast as the average

History

While food service workers comprise a large and respected occupational group, it is only in comparatively recent times that serving customers in public eating places has become recognized as a separate occupation. In ancient and medieval times, inns were established along main highways to provide food and lodging for travelers. Usually, the innkeeper and his family, with perhaps a few servants, were able to look after all the needs of travelers. Restaurants as we know them today hardly existed. Wealthy people did almost all their entertaining in their own homes, where they had large staffs of servants to wait on their guests.

Improved roads and transportation methods in the 18th and 19th centuries led to an increase in travel for both business and pleasure. Inns near large cities, no longer merely havens for weary travelers, became pleasant destinations for day excursions into the country. The rise of an urban middle class created a demand for restaurants where people could enjoy good food and socialize in a convivial atmosphere. More and more waiters were needed to serve the growing number of customers. In the great hotels and restaurants of Europe in the 19th century, the presentation of elegantly prepared food in a polished and gracious manner was raised to a high art.

In the United States, the increasing ease and speed of travel has contributed to a mobile population and a greater demand for commercial food service. Today, the food service industry is one of the largest and most active sectors of the nation's economy.

The Job

Food service workers have a variety of job duties depending on the size and kind of food establishment in which they are employed. In small restaurants, sandwich shops, grills, diners, fast food outlets, and cafeterias, customers are usually looking for hot food and quick service. Informal waiters, servers, and lunchroom or coffee shop counter attendants work to satisfy patrons and give them the kind of attention that will make them repeat customers. They take customers' orders, serve food and beverages, calculate bills, and sometimes collect money. Between serving customers, waiters in small establishments may clear and clean tables and counters, replenish supplies, and set up table service for future customers. When business is slow, they spend some time cleaning the serving area and equipment such as coffee machines and blenders. *Combined food preparation and serving workers* work specifically at fast food establishments. They are the people who take food and drink orders from customers at the counter or drive-through window. They also bring the ordered items to the customers and take payment. During quiet periods at the restaurant, they may be responsible for such chores as making coffee, cooking french fries, or cleaning tables. *Counter attendants* in lunchrooms, coffee shops, and diners often do some simple cooking tasks, such as making sandwiches, salads, and cold drinks, and preparing ice cream dishes. They also may have to help with such tasks as cleaning kitchen equipment, sweeping and mopping floors, and carrying out trash. Other workers in this category include cafeteria counter attendants, supervisors, canteen operators, and fountain servers.

In larger and more formal restaurants, *waiters,* or *servers,* perform essentially the same services as those working in smaller establishments, but they usually have extra duties designed to make the dining experience more enjoyable. These duties may include seating the customers, presenting them with menus, suggesting choices from the menu, informing the customers of special preparations and seasonings of food, and sometimes suggesting beverages that would complement the meal. They check to see that the correct dinnerware and utensils are on the table and try to attend to any special requests the customers may have.

Servers in expensive restaurants follow more formal and correct procedures. *Captains, headwaiters, maitre d's,* and *hosts* or *hostesses* may greet and seat the guests, take reservations over the phone, and supervise the service of the waiters. *Wine stewards* assist customers in selecting wines from the restaurant's stock.

Dining room attendants, also known as *waiters' assistants, buspersons,* or *bussers,* assist the waiters in their duties. They clear and reset tables, carry soiled dishes to the dishwashing area, carry trays of food, and clean up spilled food and broken dishes. In some restaurants, these attendants also serve water and bread and butter to customers. During slow periods, they may fill salt and pepper shakers, clean coffeepots, and do various other tasks. *Cafeteria attendants* clear and set tables, carry trays of dirty dishes to the kitchen, check supplies, and sometimes serve coffee to customers.

While dining room and cafeteria attendants assure clean and attractive table settings, *kitchen assistants* help maintain an efficient and hygienic kitchen area by cleaning food preparation and storage areas, sweeping and scrubbing floors, and removing garbage. They may also move supplies and equipment from storage to work areas, perform some simple food preparation, and wash the pots and pans used in cooking. To keep the kitchen operating smoothly, they maintain a steady supply of clean dishes by scraping food from plates, stacking dishes in and removing them from the dishwasher, polishing flatware, and removing water spots from glasses.

Requirements

HIGH SCHOOL

Applicants for jobs as waiters or other food service workers usually do not need a high school diploma. Most employers, however, favor applicants with some high school training, and graduation from high school is generally considered a personal asset, especially if you are planning a career in this industry. While in high school, take family and consumer science classes to learn about food preparation, storage, and presentation. Take basic math classes because you will frequently be dealing with money and will need to do addition, subtraction, and division. At some restaurants waiters carry a certain amount of money with them and make change for customers' bills right at the tables. To do this, you must make quick and accurate calculations in your head. English and speech classes should help you develop your communications skills, so very important for waiters to have. If you have hopes of moving into management positions or owning your own food business someday, take business and accounting classes as well.

POSTSECONDARY TRAINING

Vocational schools may offer special training courses for waiters. Special courses are sometimes offered by restaurant associations in conjunction with schools or food agencies, and many employers seek persons who have had such training.

Smaller, more informal restaurants may hire servers who are without special training or previous experience. In these situations, the necessary skills are learned on the job. Larger restaurants and those with more formal dining atmospheres usually hire only experienced waiters. Almost without exception, food counter workers, waiters' assistants, and kitchen helpers learn their skills on the job.

CERTIFICATION OR LICENSING

Food service workers almost always are required to obtain health certificates from the state Department of Public Health that certify they are free from communicable diseases, as shown by physical examination and blood tests. This is required for the protection of the general public.

The principal union for waiters, food counter workers, waiters' assistants, and kitchen helpers is the Hotel Employees and Restaurant Employees International Union (AFL-CIO); however, not all employees are union members.

OTHER REQUIREMENTS
Food service workers generally must be free from any physical disabilities that would impair their movements on the job. They must possess strong physical stamina, because the work requires many long hours of standing and walking. Waiters and food counter workers need to have a congenial temperament, patience, and the desire to please and be of service to the public. All food service workers must be neat and clean in their personal hygiene and dress. Those who serve the public should present a pleasant appearance, be able to communicate well, and be able to use basic arithmetic skills to compute customers' checks. In some restaurants that specialize in the foods of a certain country, servers might need to speak a foreign language. A good memory and persuasive skills are additional personal assets for this occupation.

Exploring

Explore this work by getting part-time or summer work as a dining room attendant, counter worker, or waiter at a restaurant, grill, or coffee shop with a casual atmosphere. Volunteer opportunities that combine some type of food service and interaction with the public may also be available in your area. Meals on Wheels, shelters serving meals, and catering services providing meals to shut-ins are all sources to consult for volunteering opportunities.

Dealing with the public is a large aspect of food service work, so get experience in this area. If you are unable to find a food service position, get a part-time or summer job as a store clerk, cashier, or other worker directly involved with the public.

Employers

The food service industry is one of the largest and most active sectors of the nation's economy. Employers include small restaurants (such as grills, sandwich shops, tearooms, soda shops, and diners), larger restaurants, hotel dining rooms, ships, trains; hospitals, schools, factories; and many other establishments where food is served.

Starting Out

People usually enter this field by applying in person for open positions. Job openings are frequently listed in newspaper advertisements, or they may be located through local offices of the state employment service or private employment agencies. The private agencies may charge a percentage fee for their placement services. In some areas where food service workers are unionized, potential employees may seek job placement assistance by contacting union offices.

Advancement

Employees may advance to better-paying jobs by transferring to larger and more formal restaurants. They also may gain better positions and higher pay as they obtain more training and experience.

In general, advancement in this field is limited. Nevertheless, waiters may earn promotions to positions as headwaiters, hosts or hostesses, captains, or other supervisors. A waiter may be promoted eventually to restaurant manager, depending on training, experience, and work performance record, as well as on the size and type of food establishment. Food counter workers can advance to cashiers, cooks, waiters, counter or fountain supervisors, or line supervisors in cafeterias. Large organizations, such as fast food or other restaurant chains, may have management training programs or less formal on-the-job training for dependable workers who have leadership ability. Promotion opportunities are much more limited for waiters' assistants and kitchen helpers. Some of them become waiters, cooks' assistants, or short-order cooks; these promotions are more likely to happen in large restaurants and institutions. Some of these higher positions require reading, writing, and arithmetic skills, which employees seeking promotion should keep in mind.

Advancement usually involves greater responsibilities and higher pay. In some cases, a promotion may mean that the employee has the chance to earn more in service tips than in actual salary increases, depending on the size, type, and location of the establishment.

Some individuals may aspire to owning their own businesses or to entering into business partnerships after they have earned and reserved some capital and gained the necessary training and experience. Knowledge of the restaurant and food service business from the inside can be a definite advantage to someone opening or buying a restaurant.

Earnings

The earnings of food service workers are determined by a number of factors, such as the type, size, and location of the food establishment, union membership, experience and training of the workers, basic wages paid, and, in some cases, tips earned. Estimating the average wage scale is therefore difficult and has a wide margin of error.

Waiters depend a great deal on tips to supplement their basic wages, which in general are relatively small. According to the U.S. Department of Labor, waiters earned a median hourly wage of $6.42 (excluding tips) in 2000. At this pay rate, a person working a 40-hour workweek on a full-time basis would earn approximately $13,350 annually. The department also reports that the highest paid 10 percent of waiters earned more than $10.15 per hour (approximately $21,110 annually) in 2000. Tips, usually ranging from 15 to 20 percent of the customers' checks, often amount to more than the actual wages, especially in the larger metropolitan areas. Naturally, waiters working in busy, expensive restaurants earned the most.

The department also reports the following figures for full-time workers in various positions. (All earnings exclude tips.) Dining room and cafeteria attendants earned a median of $6.53 per hour, which is approximately $13,580 per year. The lowest paid 10 percent earned less than $5.54 per hour, or approximately $11,520 annually. Most of these attendants' earnings come from wages, while a portion may come from tip pools that are shared with other members of the wait staff. Hosts and hostesses made a median of $6.95 per hour in 2000. This makes for an approximate yearly income of $14,460. Many hosts' and hostesses' earnings come from wages, but some may share in a tip pool with other dining room workers. Counter attendants at coffee shops, cafeterias, and other such establishments earned a median hourly wage of $6.72, or approximately $13,980 annually.

Another reason earnings vary so widely in this industry is because special laws govern the minimum wage that must be paid to tipped workers. While the federal minimum wage was $5.15 in 2001, employers under certain circumstances are allowed to pay tipped workers less than this amount. In 2001 the minimum an employer could pay tipped workers was $2.13 per hour. The yearly income for a full-time worker making this amount is approximately $4,430 without tips.

As a benefit, most businesses offer free or discounted meals to workers. Full-time workers often receive some benefits, such as health insurance and sick days.

Work Environment

Working conditions for food service workers have improved greatly, as more restaurants have been air-conditioned and modernized and many laborsaving techniques have become available. This occupational group is still subject to certain work hazards, however. These may include burns from heat and steam; cuts and injuries from knives, glassware, and other equipment; and sometimes hard falls from rushing on slippery floors. The job also requires lifting heavy trays of food, dishes, and water glasses, as well as a great deal of bending and stooping. In some cases, employees may work near steam tables or hot ovens.

Working hours vary with the place of employment. The majority of waiters work 40- to 48-hour weeks, while food counter workers, waiters' assistants, and kitchen helpers generally work fewer than 30 hours a week. Split shifts are common to cover rush hours; some employees may work the lunch and dinner shifts, for example, with a few hours off in between. This is good for students, of course, who can then plan their courses around work schedules.

Most food service workers have to work evenings, weekends, and holidays. Some holiday work may be rotated among all the employees. One day off per week is usually in the schedule. Benefits for food service workers usually include free or discounted meals during the hours when they work. Their place of employment often furnishes work uniforms.

Work in this field is physically strenuous, requiring long hours of standing and walking, carrying heavy trays or pots and pans, and lifting other types of equipment. Rush hours are hectic, particularly for those employees who serve the public, attending to several tables or customers at the same time. Hard-to-please customers can also add to the employee's stress level.

The operation of a restaurant or other food service depends on the teamwork of its employees. An even disposition and a sense of humor, especially under pressure, contribute greatly to the efficiency and pleasantness of the restaurant's operation. The ability to converse easily with customers is a major asset for those working directly with the public.

Outlook

Because work schedules can be flexible, part-time work is often available, and people need little or no training to do this work, the food service industry employs a substantial number of people. Additionally, the demand for restaurants and other eateries continues to grow as our population grows. In particular, the large and growing population of senior citizens, who often prefer to dine at restaurants offering table service from waiters, should mean a steady demand for those in this field. According to the U.S. Department of Labor, the overall outlook for those in food service should be about as fast as the average through 2010.

Many job openings will come from the need to replace workers who have left the field. Turnover is high in these jobs for a number of reasons, including the low pay, the long hours, and the large number of students and others who do this work on a temporary basis before moving on to other occupations. Some food service workers look for seasonal job opportunities in summer or winter resort areas. They may prefer to move with the seasonal trade because they can take advantage of the benefits the vacation area offers.

Jobs for beginning workers will be more plentiful in lower-priced restaurants, where employees usually work only a short time. More expensive and formal restaurants tend to hire only experienced workers. Because of the higher pay, better tips, and other benefits, the job turnover rate is lower in these establishments, which increases the competition for job openings.

The health of the economy and some world events also affect the health of this industry. In economic downturns, people tend to eat out less frequently and go to less expensive restaurants. Some events, such as the Olympics, can draw many visitors to an area and cause a small boom for eating establishments there. Other events, such as an act of terrorism, can cause people in that area to dine out less frequently for a time. Both such positive and negative events, however, generally have only a short-term effect on the industry.

For More Information

For information on job opportunities and accredited education programs, contact:
INTERNATIONAL COUNCIL ON HOTEL, RESTAURANT, AND INSTITUTIONAL EDUCATION
2613 North Parham Road, 2nd Floor
Richmond, VA 23294
Tel: 804-346-4800
Email: info@chrie.org
Web: http://chrie.org

For information on education, scholarships, and careers, contact:
NATIONAL RESTAURANT ASSOCIATION EDUCATIONAL FOUNDATION
175 West Jackson Boulevard, Suite 1500
Chicago, IL 60604-2702
Tel: 800-765-2122
Email: info@foodtrain.org
Web: http://www.nraef.org

For information on food service careers and programs in Canada, contact:
CANADIAN RESTAURANT AND FOODSERVICES ASSOCIATION
316 Bloor Street West
Toronto, ON M5S 1W5 Canada
Tel: 800-387-5649
Email: info@crfa.ca
Web: http://www.crfa.ca

Food Technologists

Overview

Food technologists, sometimes known as *food scientists*, study the physical, chemical, and biological composition of food. They develop methods for safely processing, preserving, and packaging food and search for ways to improve its flavor and nutritional value. They also conduct tests to ensure that products, from fresh produce to packaged meals, meet industry and government standards.

History

One of the earliest methods of food preservation was drying. Grains were sun- and air-dried to prevent mold growth and insect damage. Fruits and vegetables dried in the sun and meats dried and smoked over a fire were stored for use during times of need. Fruits were preserved by fermenting them into wines and vinegars, and fermented milk became curds, cheeses, and yogurts.

Methods of food preservation improved over the centuries, but there were severe limitations until the evolution of scientific methods made it possible to preserve food. By creating conditions unfavorable to the growth or survival of spoilage microorganisms and preventing deterioration by enzymes, scientists were able to extend the storage life of foods well beyond the normal period.

For most of history, people bought or traded for bulk foods, such as grain or rice, rather than prepared foods. This began to change in the early 1800s, when new methods of preserving and packaging foods were developed. The science of food technology did not, however, really develop until shortly before the American entrance into World War II. Prompted by the need to supply U.S. troops with nutritious, flavorful foods that were not only easy to transport but also kept for long periods of time, scientists around 1940 began making great advances in the preparation, preservation, and packaging of foods. By the 1950s, food science and food technology departments were being established by many universities, and food science disciplines became important and respected areas of study.

Another boost to the food technology program came with the U.S. space program; new types of foods, as well as new types of preparation, packaging, and processing were needed to feed astronauts in space.

By the late 20th century, few people still canned or preserved their own fruits and vegetables. Advances in production methods in this century have made it possible to process larger quantities of a wider range of food products. Scientists specializing in food technology have found better ways to retard spoilage, improve flavor, and provide foods that are consistent in quality, flavor, texture, and size. Innovations such as freeze drying, irradiation, and artificial coloring and flavoring have changed the way many of the foods we eat are processed and prepared. Consumer demand for an ever-increasing variety of foods has created a demand for food technologists to develop them. Foods processed in a variety of ways are readily available to the consumer and have become such an accepted part of modern life that one rarely gives a thought to the complexities involved. The safety of the process, nutrition, development of new products and production methods, and the packaging of products are all the responsibility of food technologists.

The Job

Food technologists usually specialize in one phase of food technology. About one-third are involved in research and development. A large number are employed in quality-control laboratories or in the production or processing areas of food plants. Others teach or perform basic research in colleges and universities, work in sales or management positions, or are employed as technical writers or consultants. The branches of food technology are numerous and include cereal grains, meat and poultry, fats and oils, seafood, animal foods, beverages, dairy products, flavors, sugar and starches, stabilizers, preservatives, colors, and nutritional additives.

Food technologists in basic research study the structure and composition of food and observe the changes that take place during storage or processing. The knowledge they gain may enable them to develop new sources of proteins, determine the effects of processing on microorganisms, or isolate factors that affect the flavor, appearance, or texture of foods. Technologists engaged in applied research and development have the more practical task of creating new food products and developing new processing methods. They also continue to work with existing foods to make them more nutritious and flavorful and to improve their color and texture.

A rapidly growing area of food technology is biotechnology. Food technologists in this area work with plant breeding, gene splicing, microbial fermentation, and plant cell tissue cultures to produce enhanced raw products for processing.

Foods may lose their characteristics and nutritious value during processing and storage. Food technologists seek ways to prevent this by developing improved methods for processing, production, quality control, packaging, and distribution. They conduct chemical and microbiological tests on products to be sure they conform to standards set by the government and by the food industry. They also determine the nutritive content (the amounts of sugar, starch, protein, fat, vitamins, and minerals) that federal regulations say must be printed on the labels.

Food technologists in quality-control laboratories concentrate on ensuring that foods in every stage of processing meet industry and government standards. They check to see that raw ingredients are fresh, sufficiently ripe, and suitable for processing. They conduct periodic inspections of processing line operations. They also test after processing to be sure that various enzymes are not active and that bacteria levels are low enough so the food will not spoil or be unsafe to eat.

Some technologists test new products in test kitchens or develop new processing methods in laboratory pilot plants. Others devise new methods for packaging and storing foods. To solve problems, they may confer with processing engineers, flavor experts, or packaging and marketing specialists.

In processing plants, food technologists are responsible for preparing production specifications and scheduling processing operations. They ensure that proper temperature and humidity levels are maintained in storage areas and that wastes are disposed of properly and other sanitary regulations are observed throughout the plant. They also make recommendations to management in matters relating to efficiency or economy, such as new equipment or suppliers.

Some food technologists have positions in other fields where they can apply their specialized knowledge to such areas as advertising, market research, or technical sales.

Requirements

HIGH SCHOOL
You can prepare for a technologist career by taking plenty of high school science courses. Be sure to take biology, chemistry, and physics. To get hands-on experience working with food, take family and consumer science classes. Four years of mathematics classes, English classes, computer science classes, and other college-preparatory courses are also important to take.

POSTSECONDARY TRAINING
Educational requirements for this field are high. Beginners need at least a bachelor's degree in food technology, food science, or food engineering. Some technologists hold degrees in other areas, such as chemistry, biology, engineering, agriculture, or business, and nearly half have advanced degrees. Master's degrees and doctorates are mandatory for college teaching and are usually necessary for management and research positions.

Approximately 60 school offer the course work needed to become a food technologist, and many of these programs have been approved by the Institute of Food Technologists. See the Institute's Web site (http://www.ift.org) for approved school information. Typical courses include physics, biochemistry, mathematics, microbiology, the social sciences and humanities, and business administration as well as food technology courses including food preservation, processing, sanitation, and marketing. Most of these schools also offer advanced degrees, usually in specialized areas of food technology. To successfully complete their program, candidates for a master's degree or a doctoral degree must perform extensive research and write a thesis reporting their original findings. Specialists in administrative, managerial, or regulatory areas may earn advanced degrees in business administration or in law rather than in food technology.

OTHER REQUIREMENTS
Food technologists should have analytical minds and enjoy technical work. In addition, they must be able to express themselves clearly and be detail oriented. They also must be able to work well in group situations and participate and contribute to a team effort.

Exploring

Students may be able to arrange field trips to local food processing plants and plan interviews with or lectures by experts in the field. Apart from an interest in science, and especially chemistry, the prospective food technologist may also develop an interest in cooking and in inventing their own recipes.

Because of the educational requirements for food technologists, it is not likely that students will be able to acquire actual experience while still in high school. Part-time and summer employment as workers in food processing plants, however, would provide an excellent overview of the industry. More advanced college students may have opportunities for jobs helping out in research laboratories.

Employers

Food technologists work in a wide variety of settings, including food processing plants, food ingredient plants, and food manufacturing plants. They may work in basic research, product development, processing and quality assurance, packaging, or market research. There are positions in laboratories, test kitchens, and on production lines as well as with government agencies.

Starting Out

Many schools offering degree programs in food science will also offer job placement assistance. Also, recruiters from private industry frequently conduct interviews on campus. Faculty members may be willing to grant referrals to exceptional students. Another method is to make direct application to individual companies.

Frequently, the food products with which food technologists work determine where they are employed. Those who work with meats or grains may work in the Midwest. Technologists who work with citrus fruits usually work in Florida or California. Two-thirds of all food technologists are employed by private industry. The remaining work for the federal government. Some major government employers of food technologists include the Environmental Protection Agency, National Aeronautics and Space Administration, the Food and Drug Administration, and the United States Department of Agriculture.

Advancement

For food technologists with a bachelor's degree, there are two general paths to advancement, depending on whether they work in production or in research. They may begin as quality-assurance chemists or assistant production managers and, with experience, move up to more responsible management positions. Some technologists may start as junior food chemists in the research and development laboratory of a food company and advance to section head or another research management position.

Technologists who hold master's degrees may start out as food chemists in a research and development laboratory. Those with doctorates usually begin their careers in basic research or teaching. Other food technologists may gain expertise in more specialized areas and become sensory evaluation experts or food-marketing specialists.

Earnings

Salaries for food technologists range from $20,000 to $200,000. According to the *Occupational Outlook Handbook,* median annual earnings of agricultural and food scientists were $52,160 in 2000.

Beginning food technologists with a bachelor's degree in food science or a related discipline average about $29,000 per year. The average salary for food technologists holding a master's degree in science is about $51,000 per year. Food technologists with doctoral degrees earn over $65,000 per year, while those with an M.B.A. degree can earn $75,000 per year or more.

Most food technologists will receive generous benefit plans, which usually include health insurance, life insurance, pension plans, and vacation and sick pay. Others may receive funds for continuing education.

Work Environment

Most food technologists work regular hours in clean, well-lighted, temperature-controlled offices, laboratories, or classrooms. Technologists in production and quality-control who work in processing plants may be subject to machine noise and hot or cold conditions.

Outlook

The food industry is the largest single industry in the United States and throughout the world. Because people have to eat, there will always be a need for people to develop, test, and process food products. In developed countries, the ever-present consumer demand for new and different food products means that food scientists and technologists will always be in demand.

Several factors have also created continuing demand for skilled technologists. New labeling laws enacted in the 1990s have required companies to provide detailed nutritional information on their products. The continuing trend toward more healthful eating habits has recently focused on the roles of fats, cholesterol, and salt in nutrition, and companies have rushed to create a variety of low-fat, low-sodium, fat-free, cholesterol-free, and sodium-free foods. A larger and more varied supply of wholesome and economical food is needed to satisfy current tastes. The food industry will have to produce convenience foods of greater quality for use in homes and for the food service institutions that supply airlines, restaurants, and other major customers. More technologists may be hired to research and produce new foods from modifications of wheat, corn, rice, and soybeans, such as the "meat" products made from vegetable proteins. The food industry has increased its spending in recent years for this kind of research and development and is likely to continue to do so. Developing these products, without sacrificing such important factors as taste, appearance, and texture, has produced many new opportunities for food technologists.

Food technologists will also be sought to produce new foods for poor and starving people in underdeveloped countries. Experienced technologists will use their advanced training to create new foods from such staples as rice, corn, wheat, and soybeans.

Finally, the increasing emphasis on the automation of many elements of food processing has also created a need for food technologists to adapt cooking and preparation processes to the new technology.

For More Information

For information on accredited food science programs, contact:
INSTITUTE OF FOOD TECHNOLOGISTS
525 West Van Buren, Suite 1000
Chicago, IL 60607
Tel: 312-782-8424
Email: info@ift.org
Web: http://www.ift.org

For information on issues in the food science industry, contact:
NATIONAL FOOD PROCESSORS ASSOCIATION
1350 I Street, NW, Suite 300
Washington, DC 20005
Tel: 202-639-5900
Web: http://www.nfpa-food.org

For national news on agriculture and food issues, contact:
U.S. DEPARTMENT OF AGRICULTURE
14th Street and Independence Avenue, SW
Washington, DC 20250
Web: http://www.usda.gov

Health and Regulatory Inspectors

Overview

Health and regulatory inspectors are employed by federal, state, or local governments to enforce those laws that protect public health and safety, as well as certain regulatory laws that govern, for example, labor standards, immigration, banking, and transportation. There are roughly 163,000 health and regulatory inspectors employed in the United States.

History

Federal, state, and local laws have been enacted to provide service

and protection to citizens in many areas of daily life. An important aspect of law enforcement involves setting acceptable standards in such diverse areas as quality of transportation and food storage and then providing ways to ensure that these standards are met. Government takes responsibility for public safety on many fronts, including various industries, labor standards, immigration, and preservation of the environment. Over the years, federal, state, and local governments have developed a system of regular inspection and reporting to assure these safety standards are maintained.

Rather than wait until a law has been violated, it is more efficient to employ inspectors to continuously watch the way in which standards requirements are carried out. For example, if a law requires that food be stored at a certain temperature to prevent the growth of microorganisms, regular inspections of the place where the food is stored ensure the law is followed, which is better than waiting until disease or illness occurs. Health and regulatory inspectors enforce compliance with all health and safety laws and regulations.

Many local, state, and federal agencies oversee the vast areas of inspection and regulation that are required in such a vast nation. One major employer is the U.S. Department of Health and Human Services, which was formed in 1953 as a successor to the Federal Security Agency, which had been set up in 1939 to "administer federal responsibilities in the field of health, education, and social security." In 1979, the department was organized into five main operating components, including the Public Health Service (serving the nation since 1798). It operates a myriad of health and regulatory subagencies including the Food and Drug Administration, the National Institutes of Health), and the Federal Aviation Administration. Other employers of health and regulatory inspectors include the Environmental Protection Agency, the Department of Immigration and Naturalization Services, the Department of the Interior, the Department of Agriculture, the Occupational Safety and Health Administration, and many others on the federal, state, and local levels.

The Job

Since there are so many areas that require regulation, there are different types of specialists within the field of health and regulatory inspection who determine how compliance with laws can best be met. The following is a list of some of the major kinds of inspectors employed by the government who work in food-related industries.

Food and drug inspectors check firms that produce, store, handle, and market food, drugs, and cosmetics. Packaging must be accurately labeled to list contents, and inspectors perform spot checks to confirm this. The weight or measurement of a product must also be accurate. The inspectors use scales, thermometers, chemical testing kits, container-sampling devices, ultraviolet lights, and cameras to test various substances. They look for bacteriological or chemical contamination and assemble evidence if a product is harmful to the public health or does not meet other standards.

Food inspectors are empowered by state and federal law to inspect meat, poultry, and their by-products to verify these are safe for public consumption. In a slaughterhouse the inspection team leader is always a veterinarian who can ensure that the animals are healthy. Proper sanitation, processing, packaging, and labeling are constantly inspected. Specialists concerned with raising animals for consumption and with processing meat and meat products include veterinary livestock inspectors, veterinary virus-serum inspectors, and veterinary meat inspectors.

Agricultural chemicals inspectors inspect establishments where agricultural service products such as fertilizers, pesticides, and livestock feed and medications are manufactured, marketed, and used. They may monitor distribution warehouses, retail outlets, processing plants, and private and industrial farms to collect samples of their products for analysis. If there is a violation, they gather information and samples for use as legal evidence.

Agricultural commodity graders ensure that retailers and consumers get reliable and safe commodities. They may specialize in cotton, dairy products, eggs and egg products, processed or fresh fruit or vegetables, or grains. For example, eggs must meet size and weight standards, dairy products must meet the standards set for butterfat content, and other products must meet standards of cleanliness and quality. The inspectors check product standards and issue official grading certificates. They also verify sanitation standards by means of regular inspection of plants and equipment.

Agricultural quarantine inspectors work to protect crops, forests, gardens, and livestock from the introduction and spread of plant pests and animal diseases. They inspect aircraft, ships, railway cars, and other transportation entering the United States for restricted or prohibited plant or animal materials. They also work to prevent the spread of agricultural disease from one state or one part of the country to another.

Agricultural-chemical registration specialists review and evaluate information on pesticides, fertilizers, and other products containing dangerous chemicals. If the manufacturers or distributors of the products have complied with government regulations, their applications for registration are approved.

Environmental health inspectors, also called *sanitarians,* work primarily for state and local governments to ensure that government standards of cleanliness and purity are met in food, water, and air. They may inspect processing plants, dairies, restaurants, hospitals, and other institutions. This involves the inspection of handling, processing, and serving of food and of the treatment and disposal of garbage, sewage, and refuse.

Finding the nature and cause of pollution means inspecting those places where pollution might occur, testing for pollutants, and collecting samples of air, water, waste, and soil for analysis. The environmental health inspector initiates action to stop pollution and is vigilant to ensure that offenses are not repeated. In urban situations the environmental health inspector may specialize in just one area such as industrial waste inspection, water-pollution control, or pesticide control.

Environmental health inspectors in state or local agricultural or health departments may specialize in milk and dairy production, water or air pollution, food or institutional sanitation, or occupational health.

The category of health and safety inspectors also includes health care facilities inspectors, building code inspectors, boiler inspectors, furniture and bedding inspectors, marine-cargo surveyors, and mortician investigators.

Health inspectors may travel to a variety of sites such as restaurants and hospitals. The health inspectors in a processing plant generally work solely at that site, and the same may be true of dairy product inspectors and sewage processing plant inspectors. The work involves making reports to the government regulatory agency for which the inspector works, as well as to the management of the institution or company being inspected.

Regulatory inspectors perform work similar to health inspectors because both occupations involve protecting the public by enforcing laws and regulations relating to public health and safety.

Occupational safety and health inspectors enforce the regulations of the Occupational Safety and Health Administration and of state and local governments. They are also employed in the private sector, where they have similar responsibilities. Their duties include inspecting machinery, working conditions, and equipment to ensure that proper safety precautions are used that meet government standards and regulations. Safety and health inspectors make regular visits and also respond to accident reports or complaints about a plant, factory, or other workplace by interviewing workers or management. They may suspend activity which possibly poses a threat to workers. They write reports on safety standards that have been violated and describe conditions to be corrected. They may also discuss their findings with management to see that standards will be promptly met.

Requirements

HIGH SCHOOL
The minimum education required to be a health or regulatory inspector is generally a bachelor's degree. In high school, you should take courses in biology and health. Family and consumer science will also be useful, as will courses in English and speech, because inspectors must communicate orally and in writing with the people whose facilities they are inspecting, and make reports to the agencies that employ them.

POSTSECONDARY TRAINING
The specific degree and training qualifications vary for each position and area in which inspection is done. For federal positions, a civil service examination is generally required. Education and experience in the specific field is usually necessary.

A combination of classroom and on-the-job training in inspection procedure and applicable law is the usual preparation for inspection positions at the state and local as well as the federal level. High school students should focus on general classes in speech; English, especially writing; business; computer science; and general mathematics. Those who have settled on a career path in health and regulatory inspection may focus on biology, health, chemistry, agriculture, earth science, or shop or vocational training.

Inspectors in the federal government must pass the Professional and Administrative Career Examination to work in consumer safety; alcohol, tobacco, and firearms; wage-hour compliance; occupational safety and health; and customs and immigration. A bachelor's degree and three years' work experience are required to take this examination. Course work and other preparation must be related to the job. For example, applicants for food inspector positions must pass an examination based on specialized knowledge.

A bachelor's degree in the physical or biological sciences or in environmental health is required for sanitarians or environmental health inspectors.

CERTIFICATION OR LICENSING

Certification and licensing requirements vary according to the position. Following is a sampling of these requirements.

As stated previously, inspectors in the federal government must pass the Professional and Administrative Career Examination.

No written examination is required for agricultural commodity graders and quarantine inspectors, but they need experience and education in agricultural science.

A majority of states require licensing for sanitarians or environmental health inspectors.

OTHER REQUIREMENTS

Health and regulatory inspectors must be precision-minded, have an eye for detail, and be able to accept responsibility. They must be tenacious and patient as they follow each case from investigation to its conclusion. They also must be able to communicate well with others in order to reach a clear analysis of a situation and be able to report this information to a superior or co-worker. Inspectors must be able to write effective reports that convey vast amounts of information and investigative work.

Exploring

If you are interested in work as a health or regulatory inspector, you may learn more by talking with people who are employed as inspectors and with your high school counselor. Employment in a specific field during summer vacations could be valuable preparation and an opportunity to determine if a general field, such as food preparation, is of interest to you. The armed forces can provide you with valuable training and preparation in such areas as transportation.

Employers

Employers of health and regulatory inspectors include the federal government (mainly in the Departments of Agriculture, Defense, Justice, Labor, and Treasury), state and local governments, the U.S. Postal Service, insurance companies, hospitals, educational institutions, and manufacturing firms. Most environmental health inspectors work for state and local governments. The federal government employs the majority of inspectors in certain areas, such as food and agriculture, which come under the U.S. Public Health Service or the U.S. Department of Agriculture. Consumer safety is evenly divided between local government and the U.S. Food and Drug Administration. Regulatory inspectors work for the Federal Aviation Administration, Treasury Department, Department of Labor, and Department of Justice.

Starting Out

Applicants may enter the occupations by applying to take the appropriate civil service examinations. Education in specific areas may be required. Some positions require a degree or other form of training. Others need considerable on-the-job experience in the field.

The civil service commissions for state and local employment will provide information on health and regulatory inspection positions under their jurisdiction. The federal government provides information on available jobs at local offices of the employment service, at the U.S. Office of Personnel Management, and at Federal Job Information Centers. The specific agency concerned with a job area can also be contacted.

Advancement

Advancement for health and regulatory inspectors in the federal government is based on the civil service promotion and salary structure. Advancement is automatic, usually at one-year intervals, for those people whose work is satisfactory. Additional education may also contribute to advancement to supervisory positions.

Advancements for health and regulatory inspectors in state and local government and in private industry are often similar to those offered at the federal level.

Earnings

According to the U.S. Department of Labor, inspectors, testers, sorters, samplers, and weighers earned median wages of $12.22 an hour in 2000 ($25,400 annually). Earnings ranged from $7.33 to $22.21 an hour ($15,200 to $46,200 annually). Agricultural graders and sorters earned from $5.87 to $11.18 an hour, with a median of $7.11. Agricultural inspectors earned a median of $13.75 an hour, or $28,000 annually.

Occupational safety and health inspectors had median earnings of $42,750 in 2000 and salaries ranged from less than $23,780 to more than $67,760. The mean salary for compliance officers (except agriculture, construction, health and safety, and transportation) was $44,140. The mean salary for environmental science and protection technicians (including health) was $35,830.

Health and regulatory inspectors for state and local governments generally earn salaries lower than those paid by the federal government.

Health and regulatory inspectors also receive other benefits including paid vacation and sick days, health and dental insurance, pensions, and life insurance. Most inspectors enjoy the use of an official automobile and reimbursement for travel expenses.

Other health and regulatory inspectors receive additional benefits. Inspectors employed by the FDA are eligible for bonuses based on their individual performance. These range from $100 to $5,000 or 10 percent of base pay, whichever is less.

Most federal inspectors, including employees of the FDA, are eligible to take advantage of the Federal Flexible Workplace (Flexiplace) Project, which permits employees to work at home or other approved sites for a portion of the workweek.

Work Environment

Most health and regulatory inspectors should expect to travel a considerable amount of the time. They will interact with a wide variety of people from different educational and professional backgrounds. Health and regulatory inspectors sometimes work long and irregular hours. Sometimes, inspectors will experience stressful, unpleasant, and even dangerous situations. Mine inspection can be dangerous, and agricultural and food inspection may bring contact with unpleasant odors, loud noises, potentially infectious diseases, and other difficult working conditions. Agricultural commodity graders may work outside in the heat or in cool refrigeration units. They may also be required to lift heavy objects. Consumer safety inspectors may work in slaughterhouses or processing rooms or in refrigerated storage rooms. Environmental health inspectors may encounter radioactive or toxic materials or substances as they strive to make all areas of the environment safe for the average citizen.

Inspectors may face adversarial situations with individuals or organizations who feel that they do not warrant an investigation, are above the law, or are being singled out for inspection.

The work of health and regulatory inspectors is important and can be rewarding. Compensation and job security are generally good, and travel and automobile expenses are reimbursed when necessary. Inspectors can be proud that the skilled performance of their duties improves life in some way or another for every member of our society.

Outlook

Government workers are generally affected to a lesser degree by economic changes than are many other workers. However, public expectations and interest concerning the environment, safety concerns, and quality products may be offset by the continuing debate concerning oversized and ineffective government and the desire for fewer regulations and strictures on daily life.

The employment outlook for health and regulatory inspectors depends on the growth of the industries or businesses they work in. The U.S. Department of Labor expects the employment of inspectors, testers, sorters, samplers, and weighers to decline through 2010 because of increased automation of quality-control and testing procedures.

Employment of compliance officers (except agriculture, construction, health and safety, and transportation) is projected to grow more slowly than average between 2000 and 2010. Slower-than-average employment growth is also expected for agricultural inspectors, as governments at all levels are not expected to hire significant numbers of new inspectors and regulators. Similarly, slow growth is expected for graders and sorters, reflecting projections for the industries in which they work. Employment of occupational health and safety inspectors is expected to grow about as fast as the average.

Some employment growth may occur at local levels, especially in the regulation and compliance of water pollution and solid and hazardous waste disposal. Growth will also occur if more power and responsibilities are transferred to the states from the federal government. In private industry some job growth may occur as a result of increased enforcement of government regulations and company policy.

Most job opportunities will arise as a result of people retiring, transferring to other positions, and leaving the labor force for a variety of other reasons.

For More Information

For additional information, contact the following organizations:
ENVIRONMENTAL PROTECTION AGENCY
Ariel Rios Building
1200 Pennsylvania Avenue, NW
Washington, DC 20460
Tel: 202-260-2090
Web: http://www.epa.gov

OCCUPATIONAL SAFETY AND HEALTH ADMINISTRATION
U.S. Department of Labor
Office of Public Affairs, Room N3647
200 Constitution Avenue
Washington, DC 20210
Tel: 202-693-1999
Web: http://www.osha.gov

U.S. DEPARTMENT OF HEALTH AND HUMAN SERVICES

200 Independence Avenue, SW
Washington, DC 20201
Tel: 877-696-6775
Web: http://www.hhs.gov/

CANADIAN PUBLIC HEALTH ASSOCIATION

1565 Carling Avenue, Suite 400
Ottawa, Ontario KIZ 8RI Canada
Tel: 613-725-3769
Email: info@cpha.ca
Web: http://www.cpha.ca

Meat Packing Workers

Quick Facts

School Subjects
Agriculture
Biology
Technical/shop

Personal Skills
Following instructions
Mechanical/manipulative

Work Environment
Primarily indoors
Primarily one location

Minimum Education Level
High school diploma
Apprenticeship

Salary Range
$14,690 to $19,410 to $24,690+

Certification or Licensing
None available

Outlook
About as fast as the average

Overview

Meat packing workers slaughter, clean, cut, process, and package the meat from cattle, hogs, sheep, and poultry. They also process animal parts for by-products such as margarine, lard, hides, wool, soap, feed, and fertilizer. There are about 116,000 slaughterers and meatpackers employed in the United States.

History

Europeans who settled New England in the early 17th century raised their own livestock, mostly pigs. In the fall, they slaughtered the animals and packed the meat in barrels full of salt or lard to preserve it for the winter. Settlers who packed more than they could eat sold it to ships' crews and others who could not raise their own livestock. After the American Revolution, when people began to live in cities, an entire culture of people who did not raise their own food emerged, resulting in the birth of the meat packing industry.

During the next century, as settlers began to populate the western half of the country, stockyards and meat packing plants sprang up near railroad lines. Ranchers drove their cattle hundreds of miles from the ranges where they grazed to the stockyards where they were sold. Until recently, large stockyards in cities with access to many types of transportation—Chicago in particular—slaughtered and packed most of the country's meat. Advances in transportation and refrigeration, however, now have made it easier to transport meat than livestock. As a result, packing houses have been established closer to the places where cattle are bred and grazed, especially in Iowa, Kansas, Nebraska, Missouri, Texas, Minnesota, and California.

The Job

The type of work that meat packing workers perform depends on their skill level and the size of the plant in which they work. Skilled workers kill, dress, cut, and cure meats, while unskilled workers perform most of the heavy labor and less complicated tasks. In small plants workers may perform a variety of tasks, while in large plants jobs are more specialized.

First, workers must slaughter the animals. Today, following the federal standards established by the 1960 Humane Slaughter Act, they use humane methods that do not cause the animals pain. Workers called *stunners* admit a certain number of animals from a large yard into a pen, where they use electric prods, carbon dioxide, or cartridge-firing devices to knock the animals unconscious quickly. *Shacklers* then chain the animals' hind legs to hoists or conveyors that suspend them above the killing floors for slaughtering. *Animal stickers* then cut the carotid arteries of the unconscious animals and let the blood drain from the carcasses. Poultry is killed in almost the same way. *Poultry hangers* shackle and suspend live poultry from conveyors, and *poultry killers* sever the birds' jugular veins with a knife as they pass on the conveyors overhead.

Before butchering, workers remove the hair, hide, or feathers from the animals. *Steamers* spray steam on suspended hog carcasses to remove hair and dirt, while *dehairing-machine tenders* do the same thing with scalding water. *Singers* use torches to singe hair from hog carcasses. *Shavers* use knives and scrapers to remove dirt and hair from hog carcasses and prepare them for further processing. *Skinners* remove the hides of cattle, hog, and sheep carcasses using knives, while *hide pullers* remove hides using machines.

Poultry-picking machine operators use machines that remove the feathers of slaughtered poultry. They then scald the birds, wash them, and prepare them for butchering. *Poultry dressers* ready chickens for marketing.

After hides are removed, *hide trimmers* remove any fat, viscera, or ragged edges. *Depilatory painters* paint sheep skins with chemicals to loosen wool. *Wool pullers* remove wool from the pelts, sort the wool into bins according to color, texture, and length; and scrape the hides until they are free from hair.

Gambrelers and their helpers use what are called "gamb sticks" to spread the legs of animal carcasses and hang the carcasses on an overhead rail to prepare them for dressing. Next, *carcass splitters* use saws, cleavers, and knives to dismember and cut animal carcasses into large pieces before further processing. *Eviscerators* remove the intestines, internal organs, and other viscera from the carcasses and deposit them in bins. *Offal separators* separate the edible parts of the viscera, such as livers, from waste portions. In addition, they set aside certain glands that are purchased by agricultural and pharmaceutical companies to make chemicals or drugs. *Casing cleaners* clean, cure, and soak intestines for use as sausage casings. *Casing splitters* split cured casings and press them flat so they may be made into surgical sutures, violin strings, and strings for tennis rackets.

After they come off the production line, carcasses go to cooling rooms where they hang for one or two days. Later, *meatcutters,* also called *butchers,* and *apprentice meatcutters* cut the heads off carcasses and trim off bruises and blemishes. Using knives, cleavers, and power saws, they slice the sides of beef, pork, or lamb into meat cuts. *Meat trimmers* trim fat, skin, tendons, tissues, and ragged edges from meat cuts. *Meat machine peelers* and *head trimmers* trim meat and other parts from animal heads using machines or knives. *Band saw operators* handle electric band saws that cut portions from hams to prepare them for curing or smoking.

Some meat is boned in the slaughterhouse. *Meat boners* cut bones from standard cuts of meat, such as chucks, loins, and rounds, to prepare them for packing and marketing. *Poultry boners* bone cooked poultry before it is processed into frozen dinners and other products.

Meat that is not sold fresh must be preserved. Some meats are pickled, dry-cured, and smoked, while others are cooked and canned. *Pickling-solution makers* mix phosphate, nitrate, and brine solutions together to cure meat. *Picklers* immerse meats in vats of pickling solutions to cure them before they are smoked. *Picklepumpers* inject meats with curing solution using a machine that pumps the solution into the meat through needles. *Dry curers* pack pork, ham, bacon, or casings into boxes or vats with dry-curing agents such as sugar, sodium nitrate, and salt. *Smoked-meat preparers* soak and clean meats to be smoked and then hang them on conveyors to be carried to the smoke room. *Smokers* load racks and cages with meat and push them into the smokehouse. They ignite sawdust in the smokehouse burner and start fans to blow the smoke into the chamber. Smokers regulate temperatures, humidity, and time of smoking for each different batch of smoked meats. They determine when smoking is done and remove the meats to the chill room. *Cooks* then bake, boil, and deep-fat fry meats such as ham, beef, sausage, and tripe to prepare them for further processing.

Many kinds of meat are ground, chopped, or formed to make sausages and other products. To make sausages, *casing-running-machine tenders* operate machines that gather casings into stuffing-machine nozzles, ready to be stuffed. *Sausage-meat trimmers* remove meat from bones and dice it; *meat grinders* grind it; and *seasoning mixers* weigh and mix seasonings to flavor it. Next, *chopping-machine operators* tend machines that chop and mix the ground meat with the seasonings to make the "emulsion," or stuffing, for sausages and other products like bologna, meat loaves, and wieners. *Sausage makers* and *mixers* may also perform these tasks. Then *stuffers* run machines that force the emulsion into casings to make sausages and similar products. *Linkers* twist and tie sausage-filled casings to make sausage links of specified lengths; otherwise, *linking-machine operators* do this by machine. *Sausage inspectors* make sure sausages are of uniform length and firmness.

Other meats are pressed or shaped by *meat press operators, meat molders, pork-cutlet makers,* and *turkey-roll makers. Ham-rolling-machine operators* run machines that wind the binding around hams, and tiers roll and tie cuts of meat to form roasts.

After meat is processed, *scaler-packers* and *hand packagers* package meat for shipment or sale. The meat industry also employs a variety of *graders* and *inspectors,* who grade meat, skins, pelts, and hides according to sales value, quality, size, and type.

Workers with several years of experience supervise other workers in various departments. Opportunities for unskilled workers include *laborers,* who load and unload racks of meat, clean equipment, and perform various other duties as needed; and *order runners,* who take smoked meats out of bins and racks and put them on conveyors leading to packing rooms. Because meat packing plants must meet stringent sanitation requirements, *cleaning workers* also are important. They include *box-truck washers* and *equipment cleaners.*

Requirements

HIGH SCHOOL

Most meat packing workers learn their skills on the job. Therefore, even though they may eventually progress to become skilled workers, those entering the industry usually need no more than a high school education. Some employers will hire individuals with an eighth-grade education to perform certain tasks. While no special training is required, high school courses in agriculture, shop, biology, chemistry, cooking, and other food-related classes may be useful.

POSTSECONDARY TRAINING

Workers who want to advance or find better jobs may want to investigate the variety of home-study courses offered by the American Meat Institute Center for Continuing Education. This program acquaints students with the business and technology of meat packing. Lists of other trade schools and courses are available from the American Association of Meat Processors.

OTHER REQUIREMENTS

For workers required to use sharp instruments such as knives and other blades, good eyesight and excellent depth perception are exceedingly important in order to avoid injury on the job. Manual dexterity is also important for those whose job is to cut the meat.

Growing concern about the safety of meats has led employers to offer extensive training in food safety to employees. Workers must be careful when handling and processing cuts of meat to avoid possible contamination. In addition, all meat processing workers follow the guidelines established by Hazard Analysis and Critical Control Points (HACCP), a food safety production system designed to prevent food safety problems. According to the American Meat Institute, HACCP became mandatory for federally inspected U.S. meat and poultry plants beginning in 1998.

Exploring

Meat and Poultry (http://www.meatandpoultryonline.com) and *Meat Business Magazine* are valuable sources of information for people who want to explore the meat packing industry. Employees at local meat packing plants may also be willing to speak with students interested in this type of work. Beginning workers may start out in apprenticeships, learning to cut meat and perform other semiskilled tasks. Summer or part-time jobs in meat packing plants can provide valuable experience for beginners in the field.

Employers

Meat packing workers are found in a variety of settings, from wholesalers and distributors to huge plants and multinational corporations. Slaughterhouses, plants, and other places employing meat packing workers are located throughout the United States.

Starting Out

The best way to find work in meat packing is to apply directly to local plants. State employment agencies may also know of openings. Some jobs may be listed in newspaper ads. Local unions also have information about available positions.

Advancement

Entry-level workers generally start as general laborers, hide workers, or meat cutting apprentices. As they become more skilled, these workers advance to more difficult jobs. Skilled, dependable workers have the best chance of advancement, but they usually must wait until openings occur. Some workers may become supervisors, and those with seniority and a great deal of experience may eventually take jobs in the management of the plant.

Earnings

Wages paid to hourly meat and poultry industry workers vary depending on the nature of the job performed and the geographic region where plants are located. According to the Department of Labor, median annual earnings for slaughterers and meatpackers were $19,410 in 2000. Salaries ranged from less than $14,690 to more than $24,690.

Wages paid to salaried employees also vary widely depending on the size of the company and the region where a company is based. A salary survey sponsored by the AMI together with *Meat and Poultry Magazine* showed median annual salaries for key positions in meat and poultry companies as $75,300 for plant managers, $45,600 for plant quality assurance managers, $40,600 for plant safety managers, and $32,000 for plant laboratory supervisors. Many of these positions require advanced education and many years of experience.

Most production workers are paid by the hour or the week, and most work a 40-hour week. Overtime is generally available, and can significantly increase a worker's annual income; in addition to time and a half for overtime, workers also receive double pay for working on Sundays and on holidays.

Meat packing workers who are members of a union generally receive good fringe benefits, including paid vacations, sick leave, pension plans, paid holidays, and life and health insurance. These benefits may depend on the union contract in effect at the plant. Benefits can vary greatly for nonunion workers.

Work Environment

Working conditions for meat packers have improved since the introduction of unions in the first half of the century. About half of the country's meat packing workers belong to either an independent union or to the United Food and Commercial Workers International Union, AFL-CIO. Still, meat packing can be dangerous, unpleasant work. Some workers have trouble coping with the sights, sounds, and smells of slaughtering and butchering animals. Floors may be wet and slippery. Some plant areas are hot; others are cold. However, Occupational Safety and Health Administration (OSHA) rules and federal sanitation requirements control the safety and cleanliness of plants. Workers wear protective clothing to minimize the danger of cuts, slips, falls, and burns.

Outlook

The growing automation of many meat packing and processing activities is expected to reduce the need for production workers. Workers displaced by machines are usually moved to other jobs in the plant, so entering the industry as an unskilled worker has become more difficult. Because turnover among these workers is fairly high, however, there are jobs available for some entry-level workers. As they become more skilled, it may be easier for them to find work at different plants. The increased competition for positions, however, has clearly given an edge to high school graduates.

According to the U.S. Department of Labor, employment growth of lower skilled meat, poultry, and fish cutters—who work primarily in meatpacking, poultry, and fish processing plants—is expected to increase about as fast as the average for all occupations through 2010.

For More Information

For information on trade school opportunities for meat packing workers, contact the following:

AMERICAN ASSOCIATION OF MEAT PROCESSORS
PO Box 269
Elizabethtown, PA 17022
Tel: 717-367-1168
Web: http://www.aamp.com

AMERICAN MEAT INSTITUTE
1700 North Moore Street, Suite 1600
Arlington, VA 22209
Tel: 703-841-2400
Web: http://www.meatami.org

CANADIAN MEAT COUNCIL
Email: info@cmc-cvc.com
Web: http://www.cmc-cvc.com

Meatcutters

Quick Facts

School Subjects
  Biology
  Business
Personal Skills
  Following instructions
Work Environment
  Primarily indoors
  Primarily one location
Minimum Education Level
  High school diploma
  Apprenticeship
Salary Range
  $14,340 to $24,120 to $40,240+
Certification or Licensing
  Required by all states
Outlook
  Decline

Overview

Meatcutters cut animal carcasses into smaller portions and prepare meat, poultry, and fish for sale in food outlets or for cooking in hotels and restaurants. They work in slaughterhouses, food processing plants, and meat packing plants. They also work in hotels, restaurants, and retail stores such as supermarkets and groceries that sell fresh meats, where they are referred to as *butchers.* There are approximately 144,000 meatcutters employed in the United States.

History

In early America, one merchant usually performed the entire procedure of buying farm animals and then slaughtering, cutting, and marketing meat. Farm families often slaughtered their own food animals, dressing the carcasses and curing the meat so that it wouldn't spoil quickly. The first professional meat packing businesses were established in the colonies of New England; with the growth of the United States, slaughterhouses were built in the new territories, nearer to the growing numbers of livestock. In the 1800s, Cincinnati, Ohio, became an important center of hog slaughtering. Later, the construction of the railroads led Chicago, with its central location, to become the country's slaughtering capital.

At the turn of the century, working conditions at slaughtering facilities often were deplorable. The publication of Upton Sinclair's novel, *The Jungle,* which described conditions in Chicago's stockyards, led to a great public outcry and is said to have influenced the passage of the Pure Food and Drug Act of 1906, one of the first attempts to regulate the food industry in the United States. Conditions at many slaughterhouses remained a source of public disapproval for many more years, until the passage of the Humane Slaughter Act in 1960, which created requirements for the more humane slaughtering of animals.

Today, meatcutters work in more than 6,000 slaughterhouses and meat packing plants, almost all of which are federally inspected.

The Job

Meatcutters receive animal carcasses in refrigerated trucks from food distributors. For easier handling, the carcasses have already been cut into sides or quarters at the meat packing plant or central distribution center before shipping. Meatcutters first divide the carcasses into rounds, loins, and ribs, and then into serving-size portions such as roasts, steaks, and chops. Less expensive cuts and meat trimmings are cut into pieces for stewing or ground into hamburger. Meatcutters try to cut everything that can be sold or in some way used into appropriate sizes. About two-thirds of a cow can be processed as beef cuts; another one-fourth can be processed as ground beef, and about 8 percent of a cow can be used for cold cut-type products.

The large sides of beef are stored in refrigerated rooms until they are ready to be cut and packaged. In their work, meatcutters use special tools such as band saws, power cutters, butcher knives, cleavers, and electric grinders to divide animal carcasses into smaller portions. Meats intended for sale in food outlets and meat markets must then be weighed, priced, labeled, and graded according to government standards. Meatcutters also place the meat in trays, wrap the trays in plastic, and fill display cases with them.

In retail stores, meatcutters are often called butchers. They are responsible for displaying the food properly, waiting on customers, and cutting orders to meet special needs. They may also filet fish, dress poultry, make sausage, and pickle meats. Other important aspects of the job include selecting meats from wholesale distributors, keeping accurate records, and maintaining adequate inventory. Some meatcutters specialize as chicken or fish butchers.

In hotels and restaurants, meatcutters are usually referred to as *meat butchers.* Their duties involve preparing both large quantities and individual portions of meat. They may also estimate the amount of meat they need, order meat supplies, inspect and store meat upon delivery, and keep records. A *head butcher* has the responsibility of supervising the work of other butchers. To lessen the work of kitchen staff, many hotel and restaurant kitchens now buy their meats already cut into portions.

Other related occupations include *schactos,* who slaughter meat according to Jewish dietary laws, all-around butchers, and *meat dressers,* who work in slaughterhouses killing animals and preparing carcasses. This type of work resembles an assembly line more than a butcher's kitchen.

Requirements

HIGH SCHOOL
Most employers prefer applicants who have a high school diploma and the potential to develop into managers. Subjects that will help high school students in this career include business and business math, bookkeeping, home economics, and food preparation. Shop classes are also useful for helping students learn to handle and take care of tools and equipment.

POSTSECONDARY TRAINING
The majority of meatcutters acquire their skills on the job, many through apprentice programs. A few attend schools specializing in the trade, but they need additional training and experience before they can work as meatcutters. Prospective meatcutters applying for union jobs are required to complete an apprenticeship of two to three years before achieving full journeyworker status.

Trainees begin by doing odd jobs such as removing bones and fat from retail cuts. Gradually they are taught to use power tools and equipment, how to prepare various cuts of meat, poultry, and fish, and how to make sausage and cure meats. Later they may learn such things as inventory control, meat buying, and record-keeping. Those in an apprentice program must pass a meatcutting test at the end of their apprenticeship.

According to the American Meat Institute (AMI), some positions in the industry require extensive training and education. Many employees have undergraduate and graduate degrees in meat, animal, and food science. Others are experts in safety, sanitation, and industrial engineering.

CERTIFICATION OR LICENSING
Depending on local laws, a health certificate may be required. Many cutters are members of the United Food and Commercial Workers International Union.

Sanitation procedures are critical to food safety. According to the American Meat Institute, standardized sanitation procedures were required of all U.S. meat plants beginning in 1997. In addition, all meatcutters learn about Hazard Analysis and Critical Control Points (HACCP), a food safety production system designed to prevent food safety problems during the production process.

OTHER REQUIREMENTS
Important skills for this occupation are manual dexterity, good depth perception, color discrimination, and good hand-eye coordination. Above-average strength is needed to lift large, heavy sides of meat. Meatcutters who wait on customers need a pleasant personality, a neat appearance, and the ability to communicate clearly.

Exploring

Summer or part-time employment in retail food stores, wholesale food outlets, or restaurant and institutional kitchens can provide experience in or observation of meatcutting. Some vocational and trade schools offer courses in basic meatcutting techniques. Interviews with meatcutters and field trips to meat packing plants and slaughterhouses also are useful in exploring the conditions under which prospective meatcutters work.

Employers

Meatcutters work in a wide variety of settings, from small grocery stores or meat markets to huge plants or even multinational corporations. They also may work in restaurants or hotels. Some hold positions in government, inspecting meat packing industries and retail operations. Slaughterhouses, meatpacking plants, and other places employing meatcutters are located throughout the United States.

Starting Out

The usual path of entry to the meatcutting field is a job with a retail or wholesale food company that has an apprenticeship program. You may also contact the local union office to find out about these programs. After two to three years of on-the-job training (sometimes coupled with classroom work), apprentices are given a meatcutting test in the presence of their employer and, in those establishments covered by a union, a union member. Those who fail the exam may take it again at a later time. In some areas, apprentices who can pass the test may not have to complete the training program. Employees at nonunion meat packing plants do not take part in an apprenticeship program but are given on-the-job training. Information about work opportunities can be obtained from local employers, union offices, or local offices of the state employment service, as well as from newspaper ads.

Advancement

Experienced meatcutters may be promoted to supervisory positions, such as *meat department manager* in a supermarket or manager of the entire supermarket. A few become buyers for wholesalers and supermarket chains. Meatcutters working in restaurants and hotels may also become managers. Some become *grocery store managers* or open their own meat markets. Government agencies, such as the USDA, that oversee meatcutting and processing, also may use individuals with meatcutter backgrounds, though additional education and specialized training may be required.

Earnings

Earnings for meatcutters vary according to location and whether or not they are members of a union. Union meatcutters generally earn between $13 and $19 an hour, or between $27,000 and $39,000 per year. Meatcutters who work in urban areas are paid more than those in smaller cities. Beginning apprentices usually earn between 60 and 70 percent of an experienced cutter's wage, then receive increases every six months until they reach the rank of journey-workers and earn full pay. Beginning meatcutters in nonunion jobs may start at about $12,000 per year.

According to the *Occupational Outlook Handbook*, median annual earnings of butchers and meatcutters were $24,120 in 2000. The highest paid 10 percent earned more than $40,240 annually, while the lowest 10 percent earned less than $14,340. Butchers and meatcutters employed at the retail level typically earn more than do those in manufacturing. Meat, poultry, and fish cutters and trimmers typically earn less than butchers and meat cutters. In 2000, median annual earnings for these lower skilled workers were $16,760.

Work Environment

Government health and safety standards require clean and sanitary work areas. The local board of health usually is in charge of inspecting food establishments and enforcing sanitation laws. Most meatcutters work in places that are comfortable, although handling and cutting carcasses is messy, and some workers must spend their entire shift in refrigerated areas.

Meatcutters may face physical hazards from saws and other sharp instruments. Those working in slaughterhouses may develop carpal tunnel syndrome and other repetitive stress disorders if they have to repeat the same motions with their hands or arms all day long. In addition to much heavy lifting, meatcutters must stand most of the time on the job. Constant access to refrigerated areas exposes these workers to sudden temperature changes, which can increase fatigue.

Following proper safety habits and wearing protective garments eliminate much of the danger on the job. Taking care to use protective gloves and to rest when tired can help employees avoid serious injuries in the workplace.

Outlook

In recent years, the beef industry has been moving out of larger metropolitan areas such as Chicago; many meatcutting plants now are located near the commercial feedlots of Kansas, Texas, Nebraska, and Oklahoma. The center of the pork industry continues to be in the Midwest, in the states of Illinois, Nebraska, Minnesota, Iowa, and Michigan. Poultry processing jobs are most likely to be found in the southern and southeastern states, such as Arkansas, Georgia, Alabama, North Carolina, Mississippi, Tennessee, and Virginia and occasionally in the Atlantic states and California.

During the past decade the number of meatcutters has slowly declined, and the decline in their numbers is expected to continue through 2010, according to the U.S. Department of Labor. One reason is the growing practice of central cutting—that is, the butchering and wrapping of meat in one location such as a meat packing plant for distribution to other outlets. Central cutting increases efficiency by permitting cutters to specialize in certain types of meats and cuts. The trend of delivering prepackaged meat to wholesalers and retailers will result in fewer employment opportunities for meatcutters at the retail level, while many of the jobs at a central cutting plant can be performed by semiskilled workers, rather than journeyworker meatcutters.

The increasing health consciousness of the American public is another reason for the decline in demand for skilled meatcutters. The consumption of red meat has decreased as people eat larger quantities of fish and poultry. The increased consumption of poultry, which can be grown to a standard size and therefore is easier to process using automated equipment, has led to less demand for people skilled in manual meatcutting techniques.

Nevertheless, the consumer demand for meat will remain strong, and new workers will always be needed to replace older workers as they retire, change jobs, or leave the profession for other reasons.

For More Information

For information on the industry and education resources, contact:
AMERICAN ASSOCIATION OF MEAT PROCESSORS
PO Box 269
Elizabethtown, PA 17022
Tel: 717-367-1168
Web: http://www.aamp.com

This organization offers information on industry research, legislative and regulatory affairs, and education programs.
AMERICAN MEAT INSTITUTE
1700 North Moore Street, Suite 1600
Arlington, VA 22209
Tel: 703-841-2400
Web: http://www.meatami.org

This union represents workers in the meat packing industry.
UNITED FOOD AND COMMERCIAL WORKERS UNION
1775 K Street, NW
Washington, DC 20006
Tel: 202-223-3111
Web: http://www.ufcw.org

Restaurant and Food Service Managers

Overview

Restaurant and food service managers are responsible for the overall operation of businesses that serve food. Food service work includes the purchasing of a variety of food, selection of the menu, preparation of the food, and, most importantly, maintenance of health and sanitation levels. Managers oversee staffing for each task in addition to performing the business and accounting functions of restaurant operations. There are approximately 465,000 food service managers employed in the United States.

History

The word "restaurant" comes from the French word restaurer, "to restore." It is believed that the term was first used in its present sense in the 18th century by a soup vendor in Paris, who offered his customers a choice of soups, or restoratives (restaurants). The first restaurants in the United States were patterned after European restaurants and coffeehouses. During the 20th century, many innovations in the restaurant industry led to the development of new kinds of eating establishments, including the cafeteria, automat, counter-service restaurant, drive-in, and fast food chain.

The Job

Restaurant and food service managers work in restaurants ranging from elegant hotel dining rooms to fast food restaurants. They also may work in food service facilities ranging from school cafeterias to hospital food services. Whatever the setting, these managers coordinate and direct the work of the employees who prepare and serve food and perform other related functions. Restaurant managers set work schedules for wait staff and host staff. Food service managers are responsible for buying the food and equipment necessary for the operation of the restaurant or facility, and they may help with menu planning. They inspect the premises periodically to ensure compliance with health and sanitation regulations. Restaurant and food service managers perform many clerical and financial duties, such as keeping records, directing payroll operations, handling large sums of money, and taking inventories. Their work usually involves much contact with customers and vendors, such as taking suggestions, handling complaints, and creating a friendly atmosphere. Restaurant managers generally supervise any advertising or sales promotions for their operations.

In some very large restaurants and institutional food service facilities, one or more *assistant managers* and an *executive chef* or *food manager* assist the manager. These specially trained assistants oversee service in the dining room and other areas of the operation and supervise the kitchen staff and preparation of all foods served.

Restaurant and food service managers are responsible for the success of their establishments. They continually analyze every aspect of its operation and make whatever changes are needed to guarantee its profitability. These duties are common, in varying degrees, to both *owner-managers* of relatively small restaurants and to nonowner-managers who may be salaried employees in large restaurants or institutional food service facilities. The owner-manager of a restaurant is more likely to be involved in service functions, sometimes operating the cash register, waiting on tables, and performing a wide variety of tasks.

Requirements

Educational requirements for restaurant and food service managers vary greatly. In many cases, no specific requirements exist and managerial positions are filled by promoting experienced food and beverage preparation and service workers. However, as more colleges offer programs in restaurant and institutional food service management—programs that combine academic work with on-the-job experience—more restaurant and food service chains are seeking individuals with this training.

POSTSECONDARY TRAINING
More than 150 colleges and universities offer four-year programs leading to a bachelor's degree in restaurant and hotel management or institutional food service management. Some individuals qualify for management training by earning an associate's degree or other formal award below the bachelor's degree level from one of the more than 800 community and junior colleges, technical institutes, or other institutions that offer programs in these fields. Students hired as management trainees by restaurant chains and food service management companies undergo vigorous training programs.

CERTIFICATION OR LICENSING
The National Restaurant Association Educational Foundation offers a voluntary Foodservice Management Professional certification to restaurant and food service managers.

OTHER REQUIREMENTS
Experience in all areas of restaurant and food service work is an important requirement for successful managers. Managers must be familiar with the various operations of the establishment: food preparation, service operations, sanitary regulations, and financial functions.

One of the most important requirements for restaurant and food service managers is to have good business knowledge. They must possess a high degree of technical knowledge in handling business details, such as buying large items of machinery and equipment and large quantities of food. Desirable personality characteristics include poise, self-confidence, and an ability to get along with people. Managers may be on their feet for long periods, and the hours of work may be both long and irregular.

Exploring

Practical restaurant and food service experience is usually easy to get. In colleges with curriculum offerings in these areas, summer jobs in all phases of the work are available and, in some cases, required. Some restaurant and food service chains provide on-the-job training in management.

Employers

Restaurants and food service make up one of the largest and most active sectors of the nation's economy. Employers include restaurants of various sizes, hotel dining rooms, ships, trains, institutional food service facilities, and many other establishments where food is served. No matter the size or style of the establishment, managers are needed to oversee the operation and to ensure that records are kept, goals are met, and things run smoothly.

Starting Out

Many restaurants and food service facilities provide self-sponsored, on-the-job training for prospective managers. There are still cases in which people work hard and move up the ladder within the organization's workforce, finally arriving at the managerial position. More and more, people with advanced education and specialized training move directly into manager-trainee positions and then on to managerial positions.

Advancement

In large restaurants and food service organizations, promotion opportunities frequently arise for employees with knowledge of the overall operation. Experience in all aspects of the work is an important consideration for the food service employee who desires advancement. The employee with a knowledge of kitchen operations may advance from *pantry supervisor* to food manager, assistant manager, and finally restaurant or food service manager. Similar advancement is possible for dining room workers with knowledge of kitchen operations.

Advancement to executive positions is possible for managers employed by large restaurant and institutional food service chains. A good educational background and some specialized training are increasingly valuable assets to employees who hope to advance.

Earnings

The earnings of salaried restaurant and food service managers vary a great deal, depending on the type and size of the establishment. According to the *Occupational Outlook Handbook,* median annual earnings of food service managers were $31,720 in 2000. The lowest 10 percent earned less than $19,200, and the highest 10 percent earned more than $53,090. Those in charge of the largest restaurants and institutional food service facilities often earn more than $60,000. Managers of fast food restaurants average about $25,000 per year. In addition to a base salary, most managers receive bonuses based on profits, which can range from $2,000 to $7,500 a year.

Work Environment

Work environments are usually pleasant. There is usually a great deal of activity involved in preparing and serving food to large numbers of people, and managers usually work 40 to 48 hours per week. In some cafeterias, especially those located within an industry or business establishment, hours are regular, and little evening work is required. Many restaurants serve late dinners, however, necessitating the manager to remain on duty during a late-evening work period.

Many restaurants furnish meals to employees during their work hours. Annual bonuses, group plan pensions, hospitalization, medical, and other benefits may be offered to restaurant managers.

Outlook

The industry is rapidly growing and employs about 465,000 professional managers. Employment for well-qualified restaurant and food service managers will grow as fast as the average through 2010, especially for those with bachelor's or associate's degrees.

New restaurants are always opening to meet increasing demand. It has been estimated that at least 44 percent of all of the food consumed in the United States is eaten in restaurants and hotels.

Many job openings will arise from the need to replace managers retiring from the workforce. Also, as the elderly population increases, managers will be needed to staff dining rooms located in hospitals and nursing homes.

Economic downswings have a great effect on eating and drinking establishments. During a recession, people have less money to spend on luxuries such as dining out, thus hurting the restaurant business. However, greater numbers of working parents and their families are finding it convenient to eat out or purchase carryout food from a restaurant.

For More Information

For information on restaurant management careers, education, and certification, contact the following organizations:

INTERNATIONAL COUNCIL ON HOTEL, RESTAURANT, AND INSTITUTIONAL EDUCATION
2613 North Parham Road, 2nd Floor
Richmond, VA 23294
Tel: 804-346-4800
Email: info@chrie.org
Web: http://chrie.org

NATIONAL RESTAURANT ASSOCIATION EDUCATIONAL FOUNDATION
175 West Jackson Boulevard, Suite 1500
Chicago, IL 60604-2702
Tel: 800-765-2122
Web: http://www.nraef.org

CANADIAN RESTAURANT AND FOODSERVICES ASSOCIATION
316 Bloor Street West
Toronto, ON M5S 1W5 Canada
Tel: 800-387-5649
Email: info@crfa.ca
Web: http://www.crfa.ca

Supermarket Managers

Overview

Supermarket managers work in grocery stores. They manage budgets, arrange schedules, oversee human resources, lead customer service, and manage each aspect of the day-to-day business of bringing the nation's food supply to the people. According to the Food Marketing Institute, there are 127,000 stores that sell groceries across the country and often several managers at each location.

Managers include store managers, assistant store managers, courtesy booth/service desk managers, customer service managers, receiving managers, and managers of such departments as bakery, deli/food service, food court, front end, grocery, meat/seafood, frozen foods, pharmacy, and produce/floral. The size and location of the store determines how many of these management levels exist in each store. In a small, family-owned grocery, the manager and owner may be the same person.

History

The supermarket industry, in the early 1900s, was really a group of small "mom and pop" grocery stores. At most of these stores, the owners or someone in their family managed the daily operations. The typical city street of that time resembled the supermarket departments of today with each store handling its own specialty. For example, the fish market and the bakery each had an individual owner and operator.

By 1902, Kroger, now the country's largest grocer, already had 40 stores and a factory as well as a management staff to keep the growing business efficient. As Americans began purchasing more of their food and relying less on their gardens and farms, the supermarket industry grew along with the need for professionals to manage the stores.

Technological innovations have increased the duties and responsibilities of supermarket managers. Bar codes, inventory systems, and complex delivery systems have increased the need for professionals who can use these tools to run an efficient store while still remembering that customer service is of utmost importance. With profit margins low and competition high in this $365.4 billion industry (in 2000), careful business planning is imperative for each store's success.

At the beginning of the century, locally owned groceries were the norm, although some chains were already growing. However, that has changed with the rapid growth of chain supermarkets. While chains have purchased some local stores and companies, other small stores have simply gone out of business. The total number of grocery stores dropped from 150,000 in 1987 to 127,000 in 2000, according to the Food Marketing Institute.

Advances in technology will continue to alter the duties of the supermarket manager. Online grocery shopping, though in its infancy, is predicted to grow rapidly over the next few years. Qualified managers trained in the newest technology and management practices will be needed in this evolving industry.

The Job

Supermarket managers oversee a wide range of resources, both personal and professional, to do their jobs effectively. Their days are fast-paced and interesting; routine duties are often interspersed with the need to solve problems quickly and effectively.

Steve Edens is the associate manager of a Kroger supermarket in Columbus, Indiana. Like most supermarket managers, Edens works a variety of shifts and handles a range of responsibilities. Working as the liaison between the corporate office and his staff,

Edens spends time each day handling correspondence, email, and verbal and written reports.

Supermarket managers often work on more than one task at once. Edens carries a note pad and a scan gun, and pushes a cart, as he checks the floor, inventory, and departments each day. While checking the inventory, Edens uses the scan gun to check on an item that is low in stock. The scan gun lets him know if the item has been ordered. "The technology keeps getting better and better," says Edens. The average supermarket carries 49,225 different items so the technology of today helps managers to keep those items on the shelves.

You may think that managers rarely get their hands dirty, but this is not the case for Edens and other managers. Edens carries a feather duster with him as he makes his daily rounds of the store. Appearance is key for a supermarket's image as well as customer comfort, so Edens occasionally straightens and dusts as he surveys the placement of advertising material, merchandise, and other store features. The typical supermarket covers 44,843 feet, so managers must be prepared to spend a lot of time each day walking.

Planning is key for supermarket managers. They must prepare weekly schedules, which are carefully coordinated with the wage budget. The managers work with the head cashier to check and coordinate schedules. The manager and associate manager oversee an immediate staff of department heads that vary with the size and location of the store.

These department and subdepartment managers are in charge of specific areas of the store, such as the bakery and deli, frozen foods, or produce. The department managers, along with the store managers, interview prospective employees while the store managers do the actual hiring and firing of personnel. Large supermarkets may employ more than 250 people, so supermarket managers need to have good human resources training.

Department heads also handle specific promotions within their areas as well as customer service within those areas. Many store managers have previously worked as a department manager.

Promotion and advertising are also on the managers' list of responsibilities. "We always plan a week ahead on displays and sales," says Edens, noting that seasonal displays are important in the grocery industry as in any other retail industry.

One of the major responsibilities of each of the managers is customer service. Managers need to courteously and competently address the requests and complaints of store customers. "I like working with people," says Edens. "It's very satisfying to me when I can help a customer out."

Though Edens acknowledges that the compensation—both monetarily and personally—is high, he has worked many 60- to 70-hour weeks and most holidays. "I don't think I've ever had an entire three-day weekend off," says Edens. "You work most holidays." Many stores are open 24 hours a day, seven days a week, 365 days a year. With at least two managers required to be on duty at a time, supermarket managers can expect to work late nights, weekends, and holidays.

At larger stores, like the Columbus Kroger, scheduling is often easier and requires less hours from each manager since the load can be split up between a larger management staff. Managers at smaller stores should expect to work more hours, weekends, and holidays.

Frequent transfers are also common. Edens has worked at over 10 stores during his 24-year career. Though his transfers have not involved household moves, larger companies do pay moving expenses for management transfers.

Problem solving and quick thinking are key skills to being a successful supermarket manager. Delayed deliveries, snowstorms, or holidays can throw a wrench into schedules, inventory, and effective customer service. Managers need to deal with these problems as they happen while still preparing for the next day, week, and month.

Requirements

HIGH SCHOOL

Speech classes will help you build your communication skills, while business and mathematics courses will give you a good background for preparing budgets. Because reading is integral in evaluating reports and communicating with others, English classes are a must for workers in this field. Any specific classes in marketing, advertising, or statistics will also be helpful. Learning how to work well with others is important, so any classes that involve group projects or participation will help you to develop team skills.

POSTSECONDARY TRAINING

While a college degree is not required for a career in supermarket management, there is a trend toward hiring new managers straight out of college. Even for college-educated managers, stores have their own specific training programs, which may involve classes, on-site learning, and rotational training in different departments.

Some colleges offer degrees in retail management, but many people choose to major in business management to prepare for a management career. Even an associate's degree in retail or business management will give you an advantage over other applicants who only have a high school diploma.

OTHER REQUIREMENTS

Interacting with people and handling customer service is the biggest requirement of the job. According to the Food Marketing Institute, the average consumer makes 2.3 trips per week to the grocery store. With this many people in each store, serving those people with professionalism and courtesy should be the number one goal of supermarket managers.

Supermarket managers should be able to handle a fast-paced and challenging work environment, and have the ability to calmly solve unexpected and frequent problems. Besides being able to "think on their feet," supermarket managers should be able to evaluate analytical problems with budgets, schedules, and promotions.

Exploring

If you are interested in becoming a supermarket manager, get a job at a supermarket. Any job, from bagger to cashier, will help you understand the industry better. Supermarket jobs are readily available to students, and the opportunity for on-the-job experience is great.

Interview managers to discuss the things they like and do not like about their jobs. Ask them how they got started and what influenced them to choose this career. When you set up your interview be sensitive to seasonal and weather concerns. Supermarket managers are extremely busy during holidays or other times when people flock to the stores in droves.

Look ahead. Online shopping is just one of the new trends in supermarkets. Be aware of industry innovations, and evaluate how your skills might fit into this changing industry.

Take some business classes. If you love people, but can't create a budget, this is not the career for you.

Hang out at your local store. Go on a busy day and a slow one. Study what activities are taking place and how management's role changes from day to day. Get a feel for the pace to decide if you would want to spend a lot of hours in a retail atmosphere.

Employers

Kroger is the largest supermarket chain and employer, operating over 3,127 food and convenience stores in the United States in 2001. Albertson's and Safeway round out the top three chains.

There are 127,000 stores that sell groceries in the United States. Over the past 10 years, the number of chain supermarkets has grown while the number of small, independent grocers has decreased. While this makes the number of stores and employers smaller, the larger stores need a variety of management professionals for a diverse number of positions, from department managers to store managers.

Grocery stores are located in nearly every city. Though smaller cities and towns may have only one or two supermarkets to choose from, in larger cities, consumers and prospective employees have a wide selection of chains and smaller stores.

Starting Out

You won't be able to start out as a supermarket manager; some experience is usually necessary before assuming a management role. You can start as a bagger or cashier or as a management trainee. There are two basic career paths—either working through the ranks or being hired after completing a college program. Steve Edens started in the stock room and has worked in a variety of positions from cashier to department manager and now as an associate manager. Working in many areas of the store is an important part of becoming an effective manager.

"This is one of the few companies where you can start as a bag boy and become the president," says Edens. Hard work and dedication are rewarded so paying your dues is important in this career.

To be considered for a management position, grocery experience is necessary. Even other retail experience is not enough to be hired as a manager because the grocery industry has so many specific challenges that are unique to the field.

Cold call applications are readily accepted at customer service counters in most grocery stores, and larger grocers do on-campus recruiting to attract future managers. Newspaper advertisements are also used to recruit new workers for this field.

Advancement

Department managers can advance up the management ladder to store manager or associate store manager. After reaching that level, the next step in advancement is to the corporate level—becoming a unit, district, or regional manager, responsible for a number of stores. The next step at the corporate level is to vice president or director of store operations. Managers at the store level can advance and receive higher salaries by transferring to larger and higher-earning stores. Some relocations may require a move to another city, state, or region, while others simply require a bit longer or shorter commute.

Earnings

Supermarket managers are well compensated. According to the U.S. Department of Labor, general and operations managers earned a median salary of $21.21 an hour in 2000. First-line supervisors/managers of retail workers averaged $13.16 per hour in 2000. In general, starting managers can expect to make $30,000 a year. Department managers at large stores average $50,000 annually. District managers earn average salaries of $100,000 annually. These salary numbers may include bonuses which are standard in the industry. Pay is affected by management level, the size of the store, and the location.

Benefits are also good, with most major employers offering health insurance, vacation pay, and sick pay. While some supermarket workers are covered by a union, managers are not required to pay union dues and do not receive overtime pay.

Work Environment

Supermarkets are clean and brightly lit. Depending on the time of day, they may be noisy or quiet, crowded or empty. Nearly all supermarket work takes place indoors, and most managers will spend several hours on their feet walking through the store while also spending time at an office desk.

A team environment pervades the supermarket, and managers are the head of that team. They must work well independently while supervising and communicating with others.

Supermarket managers are expected to work more than 40-hour weeks and also work holidays, weekends, and late hours. Because many supermarkets are open 24 hours a day, rotating schedules are usually required. Also, calls at home and last-minute schedule changes are to be expected.

Outlook

Managers in the supermarket industry should expect growth that is slower than the average for all other occupations. While the number of stores (and managers needed to run them) is decreasing, specialization and demand will create demand for the best trained and most knowledgeable managers. "There is a big demand for qualified people," says Steve Edens. "Supermarkets need people with experience and good people skills." This growth in grocery management is due to an expanding line of inventory and specialization. Because there is strong competition in the supermarket industry, stores are creating new departments, such as restaurants, coffee shops, and video departments, to meet consumers' needs.

With total supermarket sales of $365.4 billion in 2000, the industry is huge and continues to grow as consumers spend more money on greater varieties of food and other merchandise. There will be demand for people who can manage others while mastering the latest technology. Grocery stores are often at the forefront in exploring new technologies to improve efficiency, so computer literacy and business acumen will be increasingly important.

For More Information

For industry and employment information, contact:
FOOD MARKETING INSTITUTE
655 15th Street, NW
Washington, DC 20005
Tel: 202-452-8444
Email: fmi@fmi.org
Web: http://www.fmi.org

For information on mass retail careers and a list of colleges with retail programs, contact:
INTERNATIONAL MASS RETAIL ASSOCIATION
1700 North Moore Street, Suite 2250
Arlington, VA 22209
Tel: 703-841-2300
Email: klasu@imra.org
Web: http://www.imra.org

This organization has information and education programs for independent grocers.
NATIONAL GROCERS ASSOCIATION
1005 North Glebe Road, Suite 250
Arlington, VA 20201-5758
Tel: 703-516-0700
Web: http://www.nationalgrocers.com

For general information on retail fields, contact:
NATIONAL RETAIL FEDERATION
325 7th Street, NW, Suite 1100
Washington, DC 20004
Tel: 800-673-4692
Web: http://www.nrf.com

Supermarket Workers

Overview

Supermarket workers are a diverse group. Each supermarket worker is employed in one or more areas of a grocery store, from the checkout lane to the deli counter to the back stock room. There are 3.5 million people who work as employees of food stores, according to the U.S. Bureau of Labor Statistics. Supermarkets are located in cities and towns across the nation and include large chains and locally owned stores.

History

Grocery stores have existed in the United States since the 1800s.

Those early stores did not carry a wide variety of merchandise and brands. Many specialized in one area such as bread, fish, or meat. Even these early stores needed workers to help run their businesses. At the time, the workers were less specialized; often, the same person who helped wrap the meat at a butcher shop might be found later in the day sweeping out the store.

In the early 1900s, small "mom and pop" stores opened. These stores were the beginning of the modern grocery industry. Soon, some of the stores expanded into chains and the role of the supermarket worker became even more important. With bigger stores, more merchandise, and more customers, more people were needed to work in the stores.

While technology has eliminated positions in other industries, the grocery industry has wisely utilized technology (like the bar code system) but has not seen a need to reduce staff. While the technology has made efficiency and customer service better, people are still needed to do most of the jobs in a grocery store. One technological change on the horizon is online grocery stores. This is a very new trend, but even online ordering involves order takers, delivery personnel, stock room personnel, inventory control, and more.

The Job

What is it like to be a supermarket worker? It really depends on who you ask. There are so many different types of work to do in a grocery that each job can be very different from the next.

One of the first positions most people think of in a grocery is the *cashier*. Cashiers are on the front lines for the store's customer service and order accuracy. Cashiers greet customers, scan merchandise, record coupons, present totals, take payments, and help to bag groceries. It is each cashier's responsibility to keep his or her work area clean and to ensure that cash drawers balance at the end of the shift. If merchandise is incorrectly marked or damaged, the cashier calls the appropriate department to assist the customer.

Along with the cashiers, *clerks* help to bag the groceries, and, if necessary, help the customers transport grocery bags to their vehicles. *Courtesy clerks,* sometimes called *bag boys* or *baggers,* also collect carts from the parking lot and help provide maintenance for those carts.

Stock personnel play an important behind-the-scenes role in supermarkets. They help unload trucks, inspect merchandise, stock shelves, and track inventory. If you visit a grocery late at night, you can see these workers busily preparing for the next day's customers.

One of the trends in the grocery industry is specialization. The supermarket industry is very competitive, so stores are adding more services and conveniences to attract and keep customers. Some of the specialized departments have historically been a part of grocery stores, such as bakeries and meat markets, while others, such as restaurants and baby-sitting services, are new.

Each area requires workers with specialized knowledge and training as well as experience in the grocery industry. Butchers, bakers, and deli workers are generally dedicated to their individual departments in the store while other workers may "float" to the areas where they are needed.

Other supermarket workers are responsible for certain areas such as produce or dairy. While there is no preparation work involved such as there is in the bakery or deli departments, these workers regularly inspect merchandise, check expiration dates, and maintain displays.

Many supermarkets now include a restaurant or food court which require food preparers, servers, wait staff, and chefs.

Many larger chain supermarkets have a pharmacy on-site. *Pharmacists* fill prescriptions for customers, as well as offer counseling on both prescription and over-the-counter medications. *Pharmacy technicians* assist the pharmacist by filling prescriptions, taking inventory, and handling the cash register.

There are also many specialized support positions in supermarkets. *Store detectives* assist with security measures and loss prevention. *Human resource workers* handle personnel-related issues, such as recruiting and training, benefits administration, labor relations, and salary administration. These are very important members of the supermarket team since the average large grocery store employs 250 people. Supermarkets also require qualified accounting and finance workers, advertising workers, marketing workers, information technology professionals, and community and public relations professionals.

Supermarket workers report to either a department or store manager. They may have to attend weekly departmental meetings and must communicate well with their management. Because many supermarket workers deal directly with the customers, their managers depend on them to relay information about customer needs, wants, and dissatisfactions.

Many supermarket workers work part time. For workers with school, family, or other employment, hours are scheduled at the time workers are available, such as evenings and weekends. Since many grocery stores are open 24 hours a day, employees may work during the day or evening hours. Weekend hours are also important, and most grocery stores are open on holidays as well.

All of the different jobs of a supermarket worker have one very important thing in common: they are customer-driven. Grocery sales nationwide continue to climb, and customer service is highly important in the grocery business as in all retail businesses.

With that in mind, the primary responsibility of all supermarket workers is to serve the customer. Many secondary duties such as keeping work areas clean, collecting carts from the parking lot, and checking produce for freshness are also driven by this main priority.

Requirements

HIGH SCHOOL
Many workers in the supermarket industry are recent high school graduates or present high school students. There is a large turnover in the field as many workers move on to other career fields. In high school, you should take English, mathematics, business, and computer science classes to learn the basic skills to do most supermarket jobs.

POSTSECONDARY TRAINING
Postsecondary training is not required in the supermarket industry but may be encouraged for specific areas such as the bakery, or for management positions. Stores offer on-the-job training and value employees who are able to learn quickly while they work.

CERTIFICATION OR LICENSING
To protect the public's health, bakers, deli workers, and butchers are required by law in most states to possess a health certificate and undergo period physical exams. These examinations, usually given by the state board of health, make certain that the individual is free from communicable diseases and skin infections.

OTHER REQUIREMENTS
The most important requirement for a supermarket worker is the ability to work with people. "With every job I've done here, I've had to help people out," says Nick Williams, who works as a stock boy, bag boy, and cashier at Foods Plus supermarket in Columbus,

Indiana. Because workers are required to work with both the public and their own management, communication and customer service skills are important. Following directions as well as accuracy and honesty are also important qualities that supermarket workers should have to be successful.

Exploring

The best way to find out about what it's like to be a supermarket worker is to become one. Openings for high school students are usually available, and it's a great way to find out about the industry.

Take a class in a supermarket specialty you find interesting. If you think the bakery looks like fun, take a cake-decorating class and find out.

Help out with inventory. Many grocery and retail stores offer limited short-term employment (a day or two a week) for people who can help with inventory during key times of the year. This is a good opportunity to get your foot in the store without making a greater commitment.

Talk to your friends or even your parents. Chances are that at some time, they have worked in a grocery store. Find out what they liked and didn't like about the work. Another source for information is your local grocery store. Talk with the people there about their jobs.

Employers

There are 127,000 grocery stores in the United States, according to the Food Marketing Institute. This number has dropped from 10 years ago when the total number was 150,000. These grocery stores are located across the nation, in towns and cities. Some are part of a large chain such as Kroger. Kroger is the nation's largest grocer with over 3,127 stores. Albertson's and Safeway round out the top three chains. Other stores are a part of smaller chains or are independently owned.

Workers will have more employment opportunities in cities and large towns where several stores are located. In smaller towns, only one or two stores may serve the area.

Starting Out

Nick Williams got his first job in the supermarket in the same way as many others. He applied at the customer service office at the front of the store. Williams was looking for a part-time job with flexible hours and applied at several retail stores in his area.

Besides walk-in applications, groceries use newspaper ads and job drives to attract new employees. Because some of the jobs a supermarket worker may do require little education and pay a modest hourly rate, there are often openings as workers move on to other positions or career fields. If you apply in person, you should be ready to fill out application materials at the office. Neat dress and good manners are important when applying in person.

Many of today's grocery managers started out as high school clerks or cashiers. It is possible to turn a part-time job into a full-time career. "There are a lot of opportunities to learn different jobs, if you want to," says Williams.

Advancement

The opportunities to advance within a supermarket are good if you are dedicated and hard-working. It is possible, with a lot of hard work and dedication, to advance to a more specialized and better-paying position.

Supermarkets rely heavily on experienced workers, so while a college education might be helpful, it is certainly not required to advance in the field. Relevant experience and hard work are just as beneficial to advancement.

Earnings

According to the U.S. Department of Labor, the average non-supervisory food store employee made $284 per week in 2000. The following are median hourly rates for supermarket workers by specialty: cashiers, $6.99; stock clerks and order fillers, $7.94; butchers and meat cutters, $12.34; and bakers, $9.24. Some employees may make less per hour down to the current minimum wage of $5.15 per hour, while more specialized workers in departments may earn more.

Many supermarket workers are part-time employees and do not receive fringe benefits; full-time employees often receive medical benefits and vacation time. Supermarket workers often are eligible for discounts at the stores in which they work, depending on their company policy. The United Food & Commercial Workers International Union represents many supermarket workers concerning pay, benefits, and working condition issues.

Work Environment

Grocery stores are open 24 hours a day, so workers are required for a variety of shifts. Many supermarket workers are part-time employees and work a varied schedule that changes each week. Most of the work is indoors although some outdoor work may be required to deliver groceries, collect carts, and maintain outside displays. Schedules are usually prepared weekly and most include weekend work.

Supermarket workers work in shifts and must work with the managers and other workers in a supervisory environment. These managers may be within their department or within the entire store. They must follow directions and report to those managers when required.

Outlook

While the *Career Guide to Industries* (published by the U.S. Department of Labor) predicts only 6 percent growth for this industry (as compared to 15 percent for all occupations), employment for supermarket workers is good. The field has a large turnover with workers leaving to pursue other careers. Many part-time employees are seasonal and must be replaced often.

As supermarkets add more conveniences for customers, workers will be needed to staff those areas. For example, adding restaurants to supermarkets creates a need for a whole new set of food service workers.

Also, although there are fewer grocery stores, consumers are spending more on groceries. According to a study by the *Progressive Grocer,* as reported by the Food Marketing Institute, consumers spent $449 billion on groceries in 1999. Ten years earlier, that figure was $313 billion.

One reason for the decline in the actual number of grocery stores is the trend toward supermarket chains. Many small chains and local groceries have been purchased by larger chains, and others have gone out of business in the face of the competition.

The U.S. Department of Labor predicts that some occupations in this industry will enjoy stronger growth than the industry average. Bakers, food preparation workers, pharmacists, and pharmacy technicians should enjoy faster than average employment growth through 2010.

For More Information

For industry and employment information, contact:
FOOD MARKETING INSTITUTE
655 15th Street, NW
Washington, DC 20005
Tel: 202-452-8444
Web: http://www.fmi.org

For information about the retail industry, contact:
NATIONAL RETAIL FEDERATION
325 7th Street, NW, Suite 1000
Washington, DC 20004
Tel: 202-783-7971
Web: http://www.nrf.com

For information about working in retail, contact:
INTERNATIONAL MASS RETAIL ASSOCIATION
1700 North Moore Street, Suite 2250
Arlington, VA 22209
Tel: 703-841-2300
Web: http://www.imra.org

For information about union membership in the food industry, contact:
UNITED FOOD AND COMMERCIAL WORKERS INTERNATIONAL UNION
1775 K Street, NW
Washington, DC 20006
Tel: 202-223-3111
Web: http://www.ufcw.org

Index